A Separate Vision

**Isolation in Contemporary
Women's Poetry**

A Separate Vision

Deborah Pope

Louisiana State University Press
Baton Rouge and London

Designer: Barbara Werden
Typeface: Linotron Baskerville
Typesetter: G & S Typesetters, Inc.
Printer and Binder: Vail-Ballou Press

Library of Congress Cataloging in Publication Data
Pope, Deborah.
   A separate vision.

   Includes index.
   1. American poetry—Women authors—History and criticism. 2. American poetry—20th
century—History and criticism. 3. Social isolation in literature. 4. Women in literature.
I. Title.
PS151.P66   1984   811'.54'09353   84-5735
ISBN 0-8071-1159-7

   The author gratefully acknowledges permission to reprint excerpts from the following:
LOUISE BOGAN. Poems reprinted from *The Blue Estuaries*. Copyright © 1923, 1929, 1930, 1931,
1933, 1934, 1935, 1936, 1937, 1938, 1941, 1949, 1951, 1952, 1954, 1957, 1958, 1962, 1963, 1964,
1965, 1966, 1977, 1968 by Louise Bogan. Reprinted by permission of Farrar, Straus, and Giroux,
Inc. *Body of This Death, Folio, Journey Around My Room*, and *What the Woman Lived* reprinted by
permission of Ruth Limmer. *Journey Around My Room*. Copyright © 1980 by Ruth Limmer. These
selections appeared originally in *The New Yorker*. Copyright © 1978 by Ruth Limmer, executrix of
the estate of Louise Bogan. Reprinted by permission of Viking Penguin Inc. MAXINE KUMIN.
Our Ground Time Here Will Be Brief. Copyright © 1957, 1958, 1959, 1960, 1961, 1962, 1963, 1964,
1965, 1970, 1971, 1972, 1973, 1974, 1975, 1976, 1977, 1978, 1979, 1980, 1981, 1982. Reprinted by
permission of Viking Penguin Inc. Selections from *The Privilege*, copyright © 1965 by Maxine
Kumin. Reprinted by permission of Curtis Brown, Ltd. DENISE LEVERTOV. *The Double Image*.
Copyright © 1946 by Denise Levertov. Reprinted by permission of New Directions Publishing
Corporation, agents. *O Taste and See*. Copyright © 1962, 1963 by Denise Levertov Goodman. "In
Mind" was first published in *Poetry* in 1963. *The Sorrow Dance*. Copyright © 1965, 1966 by Denise
Levertov Goodman. "Olga Poems" was first published in *Poetry* in 1965 and "A Vision" was first
published in *Poetry* in 1966. *Relearning the Alphabet*. Copyright © 1967 by Denise Levertov Good-
man. First published in the *Partisan Review* in 1967. *The Freeing of the Dust*. Copyright © 1975 by
Denise Levertov. *Life in the Forest*. Copyright © 1978 by Denise Levertov. *Collected Earlier Poems,
1940–1960*. Copyright © 1957 by Denise Levertov. *The Poet in the World*. Copyright © 1973 by
Denise Levertov Goodman. ADRIENNE RICH. *Snapshots of a Daughter-in-Law*, copyright © 1963 by
Adrienne Rich; *Necessities of Life*, 1966, copyright © 1966 by Adrienne Rich; *Leaflets*, copyright
© 1969 by Adrienne Rich; *The Will to Change*, copyright © 1971 by Adrienne Rich; *Diving into
the Wreck*, copyright © 1973 by Adrienne Rich; *Poems: Selected and New, 1950–1974*, copyright
© 1975 by Adrienne Rich; *The Dream of a Common Language*, copyright © 1975 by Adrienne Rich;
On Lies, Secrets, and Silence: Selected Poems, 1966–1978, copyright © 1979 by Adrienne Rich; *Of
Woman Born: Motherhood as Experience and Institution*, copyright © 1976 by Adrienne Rich. All
reprinted by permission of Adrienne Rich and W. W. Norton & Company. Excerpts from *Of
Woman Born* and *On Lies, Secrets, and Silence* reprinted also by permission of Virago Press, London.

Publication of this book has been assisted by a grant
from the Andrew W. Mellon Foundation.

To my family

CONTENTS

A Separate Vision

Taking us by and large, we're a queer lot
We women who write poetry. And when you think
How few of us there've been, it's queerer still.

AMY LOWELL
"The Sisters"

Not that it is done well, but
that it is done at all? Yes, think
of the odds! or shrug them off forever.
This luxury of the precocious child,
Time's precious chronic invalid,—
would we, darlings, resign it if we could?
Our blight has been our sinecure:
mere talent was enough for us—
glitter in fragments and rough drafts.

Sigh no more, ladies.
                              Time is male
and in his cups drinks to the fair.
Bemused by gallantry, we hear
our mediocrities over-praised,
indolence read as abnegation,
slattern thought styled intuition,
every lapse forgiven, our crime
only to cast too bold a shadow
or smash the mould straight off.

ADRIENNE RICH
"Snapshots of a Daughter-in-Law"

INTRODUCTION

One of the most significant aspects of literature in this century is the emergence of women writers expressing a female consciousness. At no other period has there been, in sheer volume, such a literary outpouring by women. Women's literature is perhaps the major force in the contemporary period. If it is indeed true that women have been "the custodians of the world's best kept secret,/ Merely the private lives of one-half of humanity," it is natural to ask, given the existence of this material, to what extent our knowledge of literary techniques and formulations has been incomplete or shortsighted.[1] A reexamination of our familiar conceptions of theme, form, tradition, imagery, and style is in order; it is, for present critical work, both an exciting and necessary task. This study uses one of the constant themes of literature—the theme of isolation, of the outsider or peripheral belonger—to determine the ways in which contemporary American women's poetry qualifies or extends our understanding of the alienated human sensibility as it has been described by men.

Given the limitations that have traditionally existed for women, it is not surprising to find isolation a prominent feature of women's poetry. Powerful social, political, and sexual constraints have long urged a secondary role on women and acted against their struggle for full adulthood and personal realization. These constraints are evident in nearly every sphere of life, from tangible historical considerations—suffrage, property and marriage laws, access to education and professions, wage and benefits provisions, politics of medicine and childbirth, restriction to the domestic arena—to the more subtle but powerful pressures of cultural myths of passivity and sexual exploitation, religious sanctions, literary models, and the promulgations of doctors, lawyers, merchants, and chiefs who have all had their say on "the woman question." Through it all, what seems true is simply that a woman is "a person

1. From Carolyn Kizer, "Pro Femina," *Knock Upon Silence* (New York, 1963), 39–49.

defined not by struggling development of her brain or her will or her spirit, but rather by her child-bearing properties and her status as companion to men who make, and do, and rule the earth."[2] It is little wonder that when women artists come to the task of rendering their experience, they come with a profound sense of their own marginality and distance from having a meaningful impact on, or self-defined role in, the world.

The situation of women artists is emblematic of the special isolation of all women. Historically, they have lacked, been denied, opportunity. As a case in point, Linda Nochlin, in her trenchant essay, "Why Have There Been No Great Women Artists?" breaks down the circular logic of that question and conducts a paradigmatic contextual investigation exposing the degree to which women, by law and by custom, had little or no access to artistic training, materials, professional opportunities, prize competitions, studios, guilds, throughout the great periods of art.[3] Artists, such as Judy Chicago in her autobiographical *Through the Flower*, suggest that the situation has not significantly altered. Connected to the lack of opportunity and training is the fact that women have been denied a judicious, objective critical climate. In her pioneering essay on women artists, *A Room of One's Own*, Virginia Woolf wrote eloquently of the distortion and intellectual abuse a woman's work was likely to receive from a male critical and publishing establishment.[4] Her central contentions, which another critic has termed "the perpetual dancing dog phenomenon," have been spoken to repeatedly by subsequent scholars and writers, such as Carol Ohmann in her work on the critical reception of *Wuthering Heights*, Mary Ellman in *Thinking About Women*, and many others.[5] Speaking of the pervasive presence

2. Vivian Gornick and Barbara K. Moran (eds.), *Woman in Sexist Society: Studies in Power and Powerlessness* (New York, 1971), xii.
3. Linda Nochlin, "Why Have There Been No Great Women Artists?," in Thomas B. Hess and Elizabeth Baker (eds.), *Art and Sexual Politics* (New York, 1973), 1–39.
4. Virginia Woolf, *A Room of One's Own* (New York, 1957).
5. Cynthia Ozick, "Women and Creativity: The Demise of the Dancing Dog," in Gornick and Moran (eds.), *Women in Sexist Society*, 307–322; Carol Ohmann, "Emily Bronte in the Hands of Male Critics," *College English*, XXXII (1971), 60–67; Mary Ellman, *Thinking About Women* (New York, 1968); see also Elaine Showalter, "Women Writers and the Double Standard," in Gornick and Moran (eds.), *Women in Sexist Society*, 323–43; Margaret Atwood, "Paradoxes and Dilemmas: The Woman as Writer," in Jeanette Webber and Joan Grumman (eds.), *Woman as Writer* (Boston, 1978), 177–87; Ravenna Helson, "Inner Reality of Woman," *Arts in Society*, XI (1974), 25–36.

of male critical and artistic norms that confront the female writer, Adrienne Rich ironically notes its influence on Woolf herself even when she is speaking out against it.

> the specter of . . . male judgment, along with the active discouragement and thwarting of her needs by a culture controlled by males, has created problems for the woman writer: problems of contact with herself, problems of language and style, problems of energy and survival. In rereading Virginia Woolf's *A Room of One's Own* for the first time in some years, I was astonished at the sense of effort, of pains taken, of dogged tentativeness in the tone of that essay. . . . Virginia Woolf is addressing an audience of women, but she is acutely conscious— as she always was—of being overheard by men . . . she was trying to sound as cool as Jane Austen, as Olympian as Shakespeare, because that is the way men of culture thought a writer should sound. No male writer has written primarily or even largely for women, or with the sense of women's criticism as a consideration when he chooses his materials, his theme, his language. But to a greater or lesser extent, every woman writer has written for men even when, like Virginia Woolf, she was supposedly addressing women.[6]

Interrelated with the inhibitions and misrepresentations is the consideration that women have lacked a wealth of subject matter based on the viability of their lives. Every woman writer has had to deal with the realization that men write out of experience that is "universal" but that her experience is likely to be regarded as trivial and private. If the highest praise is the proverbial accolade "she writes like a man," it becomes necessary for a woman to overcome her sex to write. A man has only to express his. Louise Bernikow notes, "A woman poet constantly pits herself against cultural expectations of 'womanhood' and 'women's writing.' She gives her imagination and courage to that struggle, pours energy into it in ways that do not exist for men. Anger is approached, backed away from, returned to. Woman-ness is sometimes seen as au-

---

6. Adrienne Rich, "When We Dead Awaken: Writing as Re-vision," in Barbara Charlesworth Gelpi and Albert Gelpi (eds.), *Adrienne Rich's Poetry* (New York, 1975), 92.

thenticity, the essence to be distilled in the poems. Sometimes it appears as a blemish, the thing to be covered by the poems."[7] The result, as another critic states, is that "women frequently go to self-crippling, self-denying, self-distorting lengths to force themselves into the [male-sanctioned] mold. They are in effect involved in a struggle to 'cure' themselves of personhood."[8]

Muriel Rukeyser, Adrienne Rich, and others have acknowledged altering pronouns in their early work in order to conform to the accepted sense of the more significant *he*, even though the subjects and the experiences they referred to were female.[9] Woolf admits the extent of women's censorship of their experience in her delineation of the "angel in the house," that presiding figure of unimpeachable femininity and propriety who sabotages a woman's efforts to deal honestly with her feelings. Woolf believed that, until a woman writer could "kill" her "angel," she would be incomplete in her artistry, hypocritical about her truths. She writes, in "Professions for Women": "She had thought of something, something about the body, about the passions, which was unfitting for her as a woman to say. Men, her reason told her, would be shocked. The consciousness of what men will say of a woman who speaks the truth about her passions had roused her from her artist's state of unconsciousness."[10]

This "compulsive niceness, the curse of female socialization, is the perennial enemy of the female artist."[11] The conspiracy of silence about women's experience becomes entrenched when women artists, to be accepted, ironically "reinforce female shame by not discussing women's deviation from the cultural myths of what is supposed to be feminine."[12] Yet even "if one woman told the truth about her life,"

7. Louise Bernikow, "Introduction," in Berkinow (ed.), *The World Split Open: Four Centuries of Women Poets in England and America, 1551–1950* (New York, 1974), 8.

8. Susan Koppelman Cornillon, "The Fiction of Fiction," in Cornillon (ed.), *Images of Women in Fiction* (Bowling Green, Ohio, 1973), 114.

9. See note to the poem "Afterward" in Gelpi and Gelpi (eds.), *Adrienne Rich's Poetry*, 2; see also Rich's comment on the poem "Stepping Backward" in Elly Bulkin, "An Interview with Adrienne Rich," *Conditions: One* (1977), 64; see also Muriel Rukeyser's poem "The Poem as Mask," in Florence Howe and Ellen Bass (eds.), *No More Masks: An Anthology of Poems by Women* (New York, 1973), 1.

10. Quoted by Elaine Showalter, "Killing the Angel in the House: The Autonomy of Women Writers," *Antioch Review*, XXXII (1973), 340.

11. Erica Jong, "Writing as a Woman," *Book Views*, August (1978), 21.

12. Cornillon, "The Fiction of Fiction," in Cornillon (ed.), *Images of Women in Fiction*, 114.

would "the world split open" as Rukeyser suggests? In truth, very little women's writing of any power is likely to reach awareness in the minds of young people searching for the meaning of their lives. As Elaine Showalter has pointed out in her study "Women and the Literary Curriculum":

> Women students will . . . perceive that literature as it is selected to be taught, confirms what everything else in society tells them: that the masculine viewpoint is considered normative, and the feminine viewpoint divergent. In the literary curriculum the woman writer is by definition "minor," recommended perhaps, but not required; likely to be a recluse, childless, or even mad, and yet lacking the phosphorescent glamor of the doomed male artist. In short, a woman studying English literature is also studying a different culture, to which she must bring the adaptability of the anthropologist. . . . The male culture, reinforced by the presence of a male author and, usually, a male professor, is so all-encompassing that few women students can sustain the sense of a positive feminine identity in the face of it. Women students are estranged from their own experience and unable to perceive its shape and authenticity, in part because they do not see it mirrored and given resonance in literature. . . . They have no faith in the validity of their own perceptions and experiences, rarely seeing them confirmed in literature, or accepted in criticism.[13]

This isolation from their subject matter, from a sense of the importance and legitimacy of their lives, is perhaps the most insidious constraint women, and women writers, face.

In addition to being unable to regard their feminine experience as legitimate literary material, women have often been unable to use the patterns and givens available to male artists. In a witty but revealing demonstration, the writer and critic Joanna Russ sketches the following plots:

1. Two strong women battle for supremacy in the early West.

13. Elaine Showalter, "Women and the Literary Curriculum," *College English*, XXXII (1971), 856–57.

2. A young girl in Minnesota finds her womanhood by killing a
   bear.
3. An English noblewoman, vacationing in Arcadia, falls in love
   with a beautiful, modest young shepherd. But duty calls; she
   must return to the court of Elizabeth I to wage war on Spain.
   Just in time the shepherd lad is revealed as the long-lost son
   of the Queen of a neighboring country; the lovers are united
   and our heroine carries off her husband and lad-in-waiting
   to the King of England.
4. A phosphorescently doomed poetess sponges off her husband and drinks herself to death, thus alienating the community of Philistines and businesswomen who would have
   continued to give her lecture dates.

Russ continues, but her point is made in the humor that greets such
summaries. In their usual form, with male protagonists, "it is probably
most accurate to call these plot-patterns *myths*. They are dramatic em-
bodiments of what a culture believes to be true." As Russ asks, "How
can women writers possibly use such myths?"[14]

Additionally, in the female *Bildungsroman*, there is no return to society at the end for the fully developed mature quester. To assume her
"natural" place upon initiation into the realities and exigencies of the
world is for her to regress—to grow down and not up.[15] For her to at-
tain knowledge and self-realization is necessarily to find herself outside a society that ritually and actually enacts loss of self for women.
Similarly, in modern confessional poetry, as an extension of the Adamic
tradition, the stance of Everyman is readily available to the male poet.
It is expected that, personally alienated and desperate as his voice may
be, it is still the voice of his time. By articulating the personal psychoses
of his experience, he is simultaneously relaying the social fabric of his
world. Yet, for the female confessional poet, there is not the same extension. She is not Everyman, and is hardly Everywoman.[16] Her expe-

14. Joanna Russ, "What Can a Heroine Do?," in Cornillon (ed.), *Images of Women in
Fiction*, 3–5.
15. For fuller analysis of this, see chapter entitled "The Novel of Development," in
Annis Pratt, *Archetypal Patterns in Women's Fiction* (Bloomington, Ind., 1981).
16. Sandra Gilbert, "'My Name is Darkness': The Poetry of Self-Definition," *Contemporary Literature*, XIX (1978), 443–57.

rience only serves to reinforce her sense of isolation and freakishness. She cannot even believe in a solidarity and community with other women. Although in a very real sense male confessional poets do bespeak the trauma of their times, poets like Sylvia Plath and Anne Sexton remain individual "crazy women."

Rich even questions whether estrangement from recording her experience creates an isolation from language itself.

> In a world where language and naming is power, silence is oppression, is violence. . . . In the false names of love, motherhood, natural law—false because they have not been defined by us to whom they are applied—women in patriarchy have been withheld from building a common world, except in enclaves, or through coded messages. . . . In denying the validity of women's experience, in pretending to stand for "the human," masculine subjectivity tries to force us to name our truths in an alien language, to dilute them; we are constantly told that the "real" problems, the ones worth working on, are those men have defined, that the problems we need to examine are trivial, unscholarly, non-existent. We are urged to separate the "personal" (our entire existence as women) from the "scholarly" or "professional."[17]

Thus, women writers have a propensity to themes of isolation based on the nature of their unique relation to the world and to the self, and when they write about isolation, they reflect the special conditions that isolate them. The greatest distinction between isolation expressed by women and that expressed by men is that women perceive their isolation as a condition determined by their sex. Men writers characteristically regard their isolation as distance from a classical past (Ezra Pound), from an Age of Faith (T. S. Eliot), or from a vitalistic nature (William Carlos Williams), or simply as an existential condition (Robert Lowell and John Berryman). Whatever men are isolated from, it is not being male; indeed, their maleness is often their only source of pride and identity. It is typical for the hero of modern novels, for example,

17. Adrienne Rich, "Conditions for Work: The Common World of Women," foreword, in Sara Ruddick and Pamela Daniels (eds.), *Working It Out* (New York, 1976), xix.

to find his salvation or reality in the affirmation of simply being a man. When all else fails, the hero can always fall back on the fact of manhood, yet few women characters can fall back on the consolation that they are women.

Women do not look to a golden age in the past, because the past holds no special appeal as a time of harmony and integration for them. Their classic vocation was self-abnegation, and their orthodox posture was dependency. (The persisting image of an egalitarian green world or matriarchy in women's fiction and poetry exists more as a revisionist fantasy or future ideal than as a certifiable element in the primeval or classical period.) Likewise, the prominent myths disregard female experience and present no promise. Numerous women poets, among them Rukeyser, Rich, Edna St. Vincent Millay, Bogan, Plath, Mona Van Duyn, and Sexton, with their inventive reimagining of the female characters of folktales, legends, and myths, are more deeply interested in envisioning prototypes than in revitalizing old archetypes and stereotypes. Their energies go into rewriting and reinterpreting, giving a hitherto-unheard voice to the likes of Abishag, Penelope, Leda, Eurydice, Helen, and Cinderella, rather than returning allegiance to the traditional, received versions of these figures, whose primary distinction is in their role as consort to a man.

Women poets acknowledge the human isolation propounded by the existentialists but feel, even within this, a further isolation that is unique to the feminine gender. Simone de Beauvoir, who explored this phenomenon in her massive treatise, *The Second Sex*, refers to this as *altérité*, or 'otherness': "Woman is defined and differentiated with reference to man and not he with reference to her; she is the incidental, the inessential as opposed to the essential. He is the Subject, he is the Absolute—she is the Other."[18] The existentialist feels the gap between the self and other; women feel an additional distance between self and self, expressed most clearly in the subgenre of split-self poems that runs through women's poetry. This alienation from the self often takes the form of poems rejecting the physical body itself as that part which most visibly registers the entrapping femaleness.

18. Simone de Beauvoir, *The Second Sex*, trans. and ed. H. M. Parshley (New York, 1974), xix.

Among poems expressing isolation, I have established four basic variations—call them strategies, interpretations, visions. For convenience of description and subsequent reference, I have used the following terms: victimization, personalization, split-self, and validation. As models through which to explore the theme and the development of patterns of isolation in women's poetry, I have chosen four poets— Louise Bogan, Maxine Kumin, Denise Levertov, and Adrienne Rich. I have selected these poets, from many that might have been chosen, for the recognized stature of their work, the range they represent, their interest in themes of isolation, and the fact that all have done their major writing during this century, which is the period of closest attention to, and acceptance of, women's writing. That I am personally drawn to the power and depth of these poets' works, of course, has influenced my choices.

While I find isolation to be a significant, even in some cases a decisive, dimension to a particular poet's work, I do not regard my discussion as exhaustive of a poet's themes; nor does the incidence of a particular variation or type of isolation translate necessarily to a judgment of a poet's development (or lack thereof) and consequent poetic quality. My interest throughout is in personal and thematic attitudes, predilections, affinities, and patterns among poets and across time— the time of an individual's writing life and the nearly three quarters of a century of a full flowering of women's creative expression. Thus, while the exploration and close reading are often particular and local, the scope here is ultimately larger and more comprehensive, for the value of this study lies in its delineation of a descriptive structure that enables comparisons and analysis among a wide diversity of voices and styles in contemporary writing.

The term *isolation*, as I have used it herein, is to be understood in the context of the private and cultural situation of women, as distinct from temporary or idiosyncratic states of solitude or loneliness. It is meant to convey an essential, far-reaching sense of psychic alienation and marginality, extending indefinitely as a fundamental condition of existence. The four variations I have proposed as a way of understanding this theme evolve according to the poet-speaker's sense of the source of isolation, her self-image, and her response to isolation. These characteristics, in turn, carry implications for imagery, subject matter, tone, style, and voice. These four variations not only occur generally in women's poetry but also appear with some predictability at various stages in the development of individual poets. To a general extent, the stages form a spectrum from internalization to externalization in the poet's perception of isolation, with victimization standing at the negative end and validation being reached only after earlier stages are, if only briefly, transited.

Poems of *victimization*, as the term suggests, evoke the most comprehensive isolation, the least subject to mitigation because the speaker perceives her situation as an a priori condition of gender: femaleness itself as a constitutional flaw. Bogan's work is representative of this type, most transparently in her devastating poem "Women." Because existence as a woman is not open to change or appeal, the speakers in such poems convey powerlessness and extreme bitterness. And, since the physical self is the most visible aspect of gender, a large number of poems in this category express alienation from the body, particularly the sexual body. By extension, there is frequently an isolation from nature in its fertile manifestations, and from time as a realm of process and cycles. There is also a tendency toward a posture of renunciation. Thus, images of barrenness, usually indicated by fall and winter landscapes, dominate. The style is likely to be that of the lyric—that is, private, essential speech—lifting the moment out of the context of time. Formal rhyme and meter often reinforce the sense of a tight, closed world.

Perhaps the most interesting expression of isolation in poems of victimization is the position of the speakers. An inordinate number are literally being held immobile, trapped, or enclosed in a variety of ways, and many are prone as well. The speakers' position becomes an important indication of how they feel about themselves and their relation to the world—restricted, vulnerable, and weak. Landscapes and situations thus tend to be stylized; there is little sense of realistic events or interaction. The speakers are observers; without any sphere of movement, they lack impact on their surroundings. The poems depict a hopeless world, cut off from nature, time, others, and the self.

I have termed a second expression of isolation *personalization* to indicate that this type is based less in gender per se and more in estrangements growing out of one's familial and social experiences.

Kumin exemplifies this position in her poems that explore her alienation from her mother, her traumas both as a daughter and as a mother
with daughters, and her inability to find connection with male sexuality. Thus located in time, in a context of relationships, isolation now
has more logic than tends to be true in poems of victimization, while
remaining rooted in peculiarly feminine awareness. There is less projection of alienation onto the landscape. In fact, personae frequently
turn toward nature as a compensation for the absence of human ties.
Especially in Kumin, a greater descriptive precision in settings and
events functions as a means of maintaining rather than stylizing her
place in the natural world. In terms of style, there is an emphasis on
narrative, a stronger sense of chronology and context, since isolation is
understood as happening in time. The tone is less bitter and more
meditative than that of the previous stance, though it is still bleak and
aggrieved. In an advance over victimization, these personae are apt to
adopt the role of muted survivors rather than victims, if only to the
extent that their situations have some logic, some personal history.

The third variation, *split-self*, deals primarily with the sense of isolation a poet feels between her social female self and her inner artistic
self. The speakers in these poems may have more sense of functioning
positively in the world, yet they do so with an awareness of duality. The
external, socially acceptable, integrated feminine woman coexists with
the internal, or rebellious, unfeminine, isolated artist who is not acceptable, acting and appearing in ways defiant of male approval. Thus,
Denise Levertov, who is capable of being a positive, even celebratory
poet of human relationships, has woven throughout her work a series
of poems describing herself as two coexistent women who are in varying degrees of tension with each other. The artist and the woman seem
necessarily estranged.

The final classification, *validation*, reverses the defeatism of the first
stage. Here the positive aspects of isolation most fully emerge, and the
condition is given value and validity as a means of freedom, even as
the foundation of an alternative world. Rich is the strongest propo-
nent of this and is the most committed feminist of the four poets. In
her prose work and her poetry, she understands women as having
been traditionally isolated from a primarily masculine culture precisely through the elements—gender, female experience, artistry—ex-

plored by the other three categories; but through redefinition, she turns that separateness to a basis for hope and vision. Her thematic concern is with a necessary isolation from what is dehumanizing and empty. Isolation may begin as an enforced condition, but it ends as a choice. Her personae express the isolation of those who are in the forefront of exploration and change. Her poetry is charged with possibility and power; the style is forceful, dramatic, full of experimentation. Her images are the least earth-connected, frequently turning away from the earth to the sky to capture the sense of isolation reimagined as freedom. Recurrent images are stars, helicopters, mountaintops, radio beams, and roof walkers. Figuratively ascendant, they reverse the imprisonment characteristic of victimization.

These four stages indicate the range and distinction of women's writing about isolation, wherein a primary awareness of gender is the determining factor in that isolation. Each poet tends to move from negative stances in her early work toward positive ones in later work. This occurs, of course, to varying degrees, and the movement through the stages is neither as far nor as dramatic for all.

At the outset of his major poetry study, *Obsessive Images*, Joseph Beach observed, "As a critic, I do not aim so much to render final judgments and deliver certificates of greatness, which is something impossible and a trifle ridiculous, as to analyze and interpret stories and poems as expressions of our humanity and as effective works of art."[19] A similar intention guides this book, with the additional hope of expanding what is understood by "our humanity" as women poets have expressed it. With Beach's cautionary note for critics, I would include Adrienne Rich's conviction "that all women's lives are important; that the lives of men cannot be understood by burying the lives of women; and that to make visible the full meaning of women's experience, to reinterpret knowledge in terms of that experience, is now the most important task of thinking."[20]

---

19. Joseph Warren Beach, *Obsessive Images: Symbolism in Poetry of the 1930's and 1940's* (Minneapolis, 1960), ix.
20. Rich, "Conditions for Work," in Ruddick and Daniels (eds.), *Working It Out*, xxiii.

1 / Music in the Granite Hill

THE POETRY OF LOUISE BOGAN

Men loved wholly beyond wisdom
Have the staff without the banner.
Like a fire in a dry thicket
Rising within women's eyes
Is the love men must return.
Heart, so subtle now, and trembling,
What a marvel to be wise,
To love never in this manner!
To be quiet in the fern
Like a thing gone dead and still,
Listening to the prisoned cricket
Shake its terrible, dissembling
Music in the granite hill.

LOUISE BOGAN
"Men Loved Wholly Beyond Wisdom"

In an early essay, which appeared in a volume titled *First Impressions*, Llwellyn Jones went straight to the heart of Louise Bogan's poetry.

> Louise Bogan presents a picture of the spiritual situation in America today of the young, sensitive self-conscious woman— of such a woman in a civilization which has theoretically made room for her as a person, but practically has not quite caught up to her yet—which does not understand her, and is often aghast at her actions, often, too, callous to her sufferings. . . . Her first volume, *Body of This Death*, is a small one, but one of concentrated poetry. As the title implies, it is the poetry of struggle against, shall we say, circumstance? Not circumstance in the gross sense of the word, but against all that stifles, diverts, and disarms life of its original intention; against the pettiness that haunts the footsteps of love, especially against the limitations, imposed and self-imposed, on women; and at the same time a cry for something positive, for something compelling.[1]

Writing in 1925, Jones had only the evidence of Bogan's first book, but his view that she took as her starting point the difficult emotional, sex-

1. Llewellyn Jones, *First Impressions: Essays on Poetry, Criticism and Prosody* (New York, 1925), 118.

ual, and spiritual experience of women, and that she did so with great integrity and skill, is a view critics and readers are only recently coming again to appreciate. Although her lyrical intensity and precision of form have long been recognized and admired, the impeccably sculpted container has tended to obscure its volatile contents. Both thematically and stylistically, Bogan's poetry must be understood in terms of her unique experience of gender, examined anew in directions set out by the farsighted Jones over fifty years ago. Bogan was indeed aware of, and compelled by, the restricted power of the few social roles available to women, and she was particularly uncompromising about the exclusively feminine nature of the roles. She was also aware of how women themselves perpetuated their situation by low aspirations, mistaken obedience, fear, ignorance, and lack of imagination; but most often she believed they fell prey to romantic illusions while in the sway of physical passion. In the power of such forces, the women Bogan portrays in her poetry are always unequals in emotional relationships, victimized by their lack of power or inner control. Their experience of love is inevitably bitter and destructive.

Thus, the need for control emerges as a major concept in her work, closely aligned with the need for a strong sense of self as a means of emotional protection and counterbalance in intimacy. The women in the poems struggle to establish a sense of selfhood and control over their emotional and social environments, which constantly operate to defeat them. Even the natural world, through the forces of fertility, time, and change, inexorably asserts its power over the self. Thus, rather than acknowledge the proximity and kinship of women to natural cycles and procreation, Bogan sees these as threatening. Images of lush growth, natural fullness, sexuality, and cycles of weather and time often provoke confusion and bitterness. Characteristically, there is an enormous tension in her poetry as the physical self squares off against the spiritual self and reality attempts to face down illusion. The emotional tenor of the writing resembles an embattled standoff, often internalized within the speaker. The result is a poetry dominated by the impulse of rejection, as nature and the sexual and emotional demands of human ties become synonymous with the loss of power, freedom, and selfhood. Her desire to protect the special vulnerabilities of women fosters a need to control and a consequent rejection of things she cannot control, including passion, seasonal change, and even the female body.

In her early work, *Body of This Death* (1923) and *Dark Summer* (1929), her most frequent objective correlative for the rejection of change is her obsession with the barren, withered landscapes of late fall and winter.[2] Nature, like the human relationships enacted against its backdrop, is overwhelmingly sterile and static. The invulnerability of the self in a landscape devoid of change and emotion serves her concept of the stoic self without illusions.

The use of nature as an emblem of rejection diminishes with her later poems in *The Sleeping Fury* (1937), *Poems and New Poems* (1941), and *The Blue Estuaries* (1968), although it remains important in her images.[3] The significant change is Bogan's increasing dependence on the mental and creative processes as spheres of selfhood and control. Poetry emerges as the containable, acceptable landscape of the self. The shift seems to be motivated by self-protection, moving away from the risk and tension of struggling with the human and physical aspects of existence. In *The Sleeping Fury*, poetry is clearly given the burden of answering the need for fulfillment and constancy unobtainable in human relationships. She reaches the point of reduction where only her mental discipline and poetic skill provide a bulwark against the external world's betrayal. The sadness is that it left her little to write about, and in her late years the quietus she had won was finally too crucial and fragile to risk in the psychic demands of her best poetry. She came to believe the muse was gone, and, regrettably, much of her work became set pieces, exercises, mere imitations of her former power. With a few beautiful, poignant exceptions, such as "After the Persian," "Song for the Last Act," and the elusive, moving journal pieces, her output after the early 1940s is small and uneven in quality.

From the beginning, Bogan is creating a study of female isolation from major aspects of human existence—the natural world, social roles, the physical body, and time. Her poems work through the process of a persona's recognition of isolation or her effort to overcome it.

2. Louise Bogan, *Body of This Death* (New York, 1923); *Dark Summer* (New York, 1929).

3. Louise Bogan, *The Sleeping Fury* (New York, 1937); *Poems and New Poems* (New York, 1941); *Collected Poems: 1923–1953* (New York, 1954); *The Blue Estuaries: Poems 1923–1968* (New York, 1968).

Bogan's term for this state is *death*; the diminishment and circumvention of the self results in a spiritual and even literal death from which the speaker seeks escape and freedom on new terms. Thus, she takes as her first collection's title and point of departure the startling epigraph from Saint Paul, "Who shall deliver me from the body of this death?"[4] With little alteration, this phrase continues to serve the entire canon. *Body of This Death* remains the most compelling of all Bogan's work, and it is the most fruitful for close reading, not only in the richness and durability of the poems, but in the poet's touching and relatively unguarded cry against necessity and her youthful determination to avoid life's traps. As such, the collection represents Bogan's range of expression of isolation and exemplifies the stance of victimization.

II

The central impulse of *Body of This Death* is escape. In terms of its epigraph and title, the book explores the meaning of "death," the means of deliverance, and the role of the body in its own oppression and release. A remarkable number of the women in the poems are bound, trapped, prone, immobile, or dead—figuratively or actually unable to express physical or emotional freedom. In poems like "Medusa," "The Frightened Man," "Knowledge," "Portrait," "My Voice Not Being Proud," and "Statue and Birds," a speaker's static outer state corresponds to an inner paralysis of will and selfhood—symptom and the cause of her isolation. Coincident with the powerlessness of the women is the passivity of the epigraph's question; the speaker behind the epigraph, unwilling or unable to deliver herself, looks elsewhere for someone or something to save her. She first reaches toward the environment, as four of the five opening poems present experiments in landscape: the desert in "A Tale," the jungle in "Decoration," the mythical realm of "Medusa," and the New England countryside in "A Letter." Escape into another person, indicative of the emotional en-

---

4. Most of the poems printed in *Body of This Death* were included in the subsequent collections *Poems and New Poems*, *Collected Poems*, and *The Blue Estuaries* with the exception of the following, which were never reprinted in Bogan's lifetime: "Decoration," "Words for Departure," "Epitaph for a Romantic Woman," "Song," and "A Letter." Ruth Limmer reprinted "A Letter," in *Journey Around My Room: The Autobiography of Louise Bogan, A Mosaic by Ruth Limmer* (New York, 1980).

vironment, is explored in such poems as "The Frightened Man," "Be-trothed," and "Words for Departure," but similarly, the escape fails. The poems at the heart of the collection, "Men Loved Wholly Beyond Wisdom" and "Women," resolve to the utterly bleak proposition that women are by gender unable to love, to move, to be free, that it is nei-ther landscapes, partners, nor roles, but women's very selves that are ultimately "the body of this death." This clearly marks the nadir of her search. Yet, in the remaining poems of the book a new energy and capacity for escape emerge. "Women" brings about the final abandon-ment of hope for deliverance from the outside. The "who" of the epi-graph can be answered only in the first person. The ultimate support-ability or even accuracy of this premise is severely tested in Bogan's life and work, as well as by the powerful poems that precede this revela-tion in *Body of This Death*. Nevertheless, the final poems evince a de-termination for positive action and responsibility that the earlier, static poems do not. Immobilization characterizes the speakers before "Women," while movement and spatialization characterize most of those following it.

The youth of the opening poem, "A Tale," is an early version of the characteristically trapped and enclosed Bogan persona. This poem es-tablishes the motif of the inner journey, or quest, which reappears in subsequent poems and which is suggested by the overall arrangement of the volume itself. Here the metaphoric movement to the interior underlies the literal geographic progression from the sea inland to a rocky desert, signaling the youth's rejection of the familiar world of time and motion in an attempt to locate a permanent, unchanging self.

> This youth too long has heard the break
> Of waters in a land of change.
> He goes to see what suns can make
> From soil more indurate and strange.
>
> He cuts what holds his days together
> And shuts him in, as lock on lock:
> The arrowed vane announcing weather,
> The tripping racket of a clock;
>
> Seeking, I think, a light that waits
> Still as a lamp upon a shelf,—

> A land with hills like rocky gates
> Where no sea leaps upon itself.

The forces frustrating him—weather, time, tides—are the stuff of dailiness, but they drive him to seek a radical reordering of landscape. What is unusual is that these conventional symbols of mundanity, dullness, and sameness are not eschewed for something more vital and lovely, but are themselves associated with other conventional symbols of fertility—water, change, sound. All these symbols are rejected in favor of silence, sterility, and absolute stillness—a desert where "no sea leaps upon itself." I suggest that this is the wish, encoded in the use of the male subject and the landscape projection, of a female persona who ambivalently regards the body, the fertile environment, as an oppressive force and who can only imagine release in terms of an utterly unproductive landscape. Yet, the youth's goal emerges not as release but as death. Short of this finality of stasis, all "he" will ever find is an opposition in the self that is both ambiguous and "dreadful."

> But he will find that nothing dares
> To be enduring, save where, south
> Of hidden deserts, torn fire glares
> On beauty with a rusted mouth,—
> Where something dreadful and another
> Look quietly upon each other.

At the center of the landscape is an embattled deadlock between the "fire" of the inner self and the "beauty" of the physical self in which the world would imprison one. This final alignment comes off with less power and direction than it might because Bogan lapses into vague, imprecise language, diminishing what should be a strong, dramatic closure. The weak use of "something," "another," "each other," undercuts the revelation of meaning, just as her use of the masculine figure and the third-person seeker obscures her personal stake in the poem. Her own participation in the experience becomes clearer in "Medusa," which functions as a sequel to "A Tale."

"Medusa" continues the previous poem's final image of a static, unproductive landscape dominated by forces "looking quietly upon each other." In order to create the ideal environment the youth sought,

Bogan turns to the figure of Medusa, whose mythic power stops time and process, seeking the goddess the way the youth seeks his desert.

> I had come to the house, in a cave of trees,
> Facing a sheer sky.
> Everything moved,—a bell hung ready to strike,
> Sun and reflection wheeled by.
>
> When the bare eyes were before me
> And the hissing hair,
> Held up at a window, seen through a door.
> The stiff bald eyes, the serpents on the forehead
> Formed in the air.

After this apparition, the speaker is frozen in a landscape that evades the death wish of the youth by virtue of its water and foliage; yet, through the agency of Medusa, any threatening process is also evaded. In this fantastic realm, the speaker has it both ways, much like the figures adorning Keats's Grecian urn. There is fertility (water, grass, hay) without the corruption of it (the water does not fall, nor the hay get mown).

> The water will always fall, and will not fall,
> And the tipped bell make no sound.
> The grass will always be growing for hay
> Deep in the ground.
>
> And I shall stand here like a shadow
> Under the great balanced day,
> My eyes on the yellow dust, that was lifting in the wind,
> And does not drift away.

This paradoxical stasis and motion is not "dreadful" to the speaker, as are the opposing forces of "A Tale"; here all has come to a "great balanced day." The drawback is that this balance is possible only through the intervention of the supernatural. At this point the speaker cannot appropriate for herself the feminine power embodied in Medusa, and so she remains still and passive in the dead scene.

"Betrothed" is a beautiful, complex poem that successfully moves away from the depersonalization and encoding of "A Tale" and "Me-

dusa" in the continuing search for a personal landscape and incorpo-
rates an exploration of personal relationships and conventional gender
ties. A young woman about to be married mourns the estrangement
from her mother and her girlhood friend that marriage seems to de-
mand. Her rite of passage into womanhood is connected with the loss
of bonds to other women, yet it is these relationships, rather than the
prospective male lover's, which she associates positively with discovery,
sensuality, and freedom. Significantly, the speaker envisions her impending separation from her friend as a change of landscapes:

> In the country whereto I go
> I shall not see the face of my friend
> Nor her hair the color of sunburnt grasses;
> Together we shall not find
> The land on whose hills bends the new moon
> In air traversed of birds.

The speaker hears in her mother's emptiness and bitter memories a
curse on her own future as wife and mother.

> My mother remembers the agony of her womb
> And long years that seemed to promise more than this.
> She says, "You do not love me,
> You do not want me,
> You will go away."

The male lover does not compensate the speaker for her real and projected losses. Their attitudes together are stiff and formal, their landscape negligible and dim. Further, the girl's perception of her lover is
disoriented; at no point is he seen as a realistic totality, but rather as a
set of disembodied features. Bogan accomplishes this depersonalization through redundancy and deliberate phrasing.

> You have put your two hands upon me, and your mouth,
> You have said my name as a prayer
>
> . . . .
>
> I have watched your eyes, cleansed from regret,
> And your lips, closed over all that love cannot say.

By contrast, the friend is perceived as a whole, rather than a collection of separate features, and it is with her that the speaker achieves intimacy and communication, while the conventions of romantic love prevent any realistic exchange with the man. Yet this recognition ultimately leaves her no less passive and imprisoned than earlier speakers, since she capitulates to the predicted course, her romantic illusions interweaving with her resignation.

> What have I thought of love?
> I have thought that it would bring me lost delights,
>   and splendor,
> As a wind out of old time. . . .

Isolated from her love and her sex, at odds with the landscape of her new role, she is also isolated from time, already seeking to recover events from the past—"lost delights," "old time"—already investing her happiness in the memory of a time that will quickly become as illusory as her expectations for the future. Therefore, the poem closes with the darkening image of the young girl under the weeping willow —almost as if she has passed already into the ironic imprisonment of a pose—the long, oval leaves trailing in the water, suggesting powerlessness and passivity.

> But there is only the evening here,
> And the sound of willows
> Now and again dipping their long oval leaves in
>   the water.

As one critic has pointed out, "Speech in the form of slow declarations empowers [the speaker] to probe the rhythms of time and change that have prompted her misgivings. . . . Bogan has . . . found in the tradition of betrothal lyric a fusion of form and language where simplicity represents an immense compression of feeling and an effort to overcome fear and conflict."[5] She inverts the convention, making it an antibetrothal poem.

5. Elizabeth Perlmutter, "A Doll's House: The Girl in the Poetry of Edna St. Vincent Millay and Louise Bogan," *Twentieth Century Literature*, XXIII (1977), 171.

The impotence and despair in "Betrothed" are dramatically developed and climaxed through the tableau formed by four poems that follow it: "Words for Departure," "Ad Castitatem," "Knowledge," and "Portrait." These poems form what amounts to a marriage sequence within the larger arrangement of *Body of This Death*, moving eloquently from the ominous ambivalence of the young girl on the verge of commitment, through the breakdown of the relationship and aggrieved separation, to a bitter renunciation of sexuality altogether, and finally to a stoic but nonetheless radical resignation to celibacy. Each step is a further armoring against the pain and betrayal of sexual commitment, concluding in the most extreme withdrawal of all, death.

The autobiographical dimension of these serial poems cannot be denied. They combine with others published contemporaneously in little magazines and journals to document frankly and compellingly the emotional turmoil of Bogan's own early marriage in 1916, when she was barely nineteen.[6] She married Curt Alexander, an army officer several years older than she, with whom she moved to the Panama Canal Zone. There her only child, Mathilde (Maidie), was born soon after. There is little account of this marriage. Bogan's collected letters, which begin in 1920, after her marriage had ended, make few references to this period. The marriage was a disaster, as Bogan acknowledged: "I was the highly charged and neurotically inclined product of an extraordinary childhood and an unfortunate early marriage, into which state I had rushed to escape the first."[7]

Her "extraordinary childhood" began in Livermore Falls, Maine, where she was born August 11, 1897, to Daniel and Mary Bogan. It was a traumatizing, unsettled household, disrupted by frequent and precipitous moves. In her journal, wherein she had undertaken the attempt to recollect and understand her early life and experience, Bogan wrote

6. Poems that center on Bogan's marriage and early widowhood but not collected in *Body of This Death* (or elsewhere) are: "The Young Wife," *Others*, IV (December, 1917); "Survival," *Measure*, No. 9 (November, 1921); a series of five poems published under the title "Beginning and End" that included "Elders," "Resolve," "Leavetaking," "To a Dead Lover," and "Knowledge" (which alone of these was reprinted in *Body of This Death*), *Poetry*, August, 1922; "The Stones," *Measure*, No. 28 (June, 1923). *Body of This Death* is hereinafter cited parenthetically in text as *BD*.

7. Louise Bogan to Morton D. Zabel, June 11, 1937, in Ruth Limmer (ed.), *What the Woman Lived: Selected Letters of Louise Bogan, 1920–1970* (New York, 1973), 6n2. Hereinafter cited parenthetically in text as *WWL*.

years later, "For people like myself to look back is a task. It is like reentering a trap, or a labyrinth, from which one has only too lately, and too narrowly, escaped. . . . I must have experienced violence from birth. But I remember it, at first, as only bound up with flight. I was bundled up and carried away."[8] Her memories of the poverty-stricken mill towns like Livermore, Milton, and Ballardvale, where she spent her youth, echo the rugged, wasted landscapes that fill her poetry. "Terre Vague—uncultivated land, filled with 'chance vegetation.' The unbuilt lots of my childhood, filled with tansy and chicory; sometimes with some scrub trees. The three-family houses abutted on them. . . . Sometimes they were sunken, between two blocks of flats, and boys played ball in them in the evening.—The edge of things; the beaten dead end of nature, that fascinated me almost with a sexual fascination" (*JAMR*, 20).

The strange resonance of "the beaten dead end of nature," so strong in Bogan's later poetry, comes out of her own early identification with physical and psychic abuse, almost certainly at the hands of her mother. It also helps to account for the destructive sense of gender and love Bogan carried into her poetry and emotional relationships. One of many revealing passages from her journal speaks to the mingled love and terror of Bogan for her mother. As a child she associated peace with her mother's sewing because the sound the needle made soothed and assured her that her mother's hands were occupied and not threatening to hurt her. "When she sewed, and that, in my childhood was rarely, I could hear the rasp of the needle against the thimble (she had a silver one), and that meant peace. For the hands that peeled the apple and measured out the encircling ribbon and lace could also deal out disorder and destruction. They could tear things to bits; put all their soft strength into thrusts and blows; they would lift objects so that they became threats of missiles. But sometimes they made that lovely noise of thimble and needle" (*JAMR*, 29). There were other tensions; Mary Bogan, apparently a very beautiful and proud woman, had other lovers while still married to Bogan's father. Bogan's letters mention little about her father, who seems to have been frequently

8. Limmer, *Journey Around My Room*. Hereinafter cited parenthetically in text as *JAMR*.

absent, a peripheral figure in his daughter's life. Her later reminiscence to Edmund Wilson, however, casts him in a negative light. "I made a visit to my own ancestral home and am beginning to understand more and more what Yeats meant by the 'Paudeen,' and why my mother was an admirable person, even if she nearly wrecked every ordinary life within sight. —She was against the pennypinchers and the logic-choppers; she loved beauty and threw everything away, and what is most important, she was filled with the strongest vitality I have ever seen. —And how the 'Paudeen,' (from which the other side of my nature unfortunately stems!) hated and feared her!" (*WWL*, 185).

In early childhood, Bogan once witnessed something connected to her parents' marital difficulties that was so traumatic she lost her sight for two days and afterward could not remember what she saw. "I remember my sight coming back, by seeing the flat forked light of the gas flame, in its etched glass shade, suddenly appearing beside the bureau. What had I seen? I shall never know" (*JAMR*, 26). She wrote to Rolfe Humphries in 1924 that her life had been "blighted *very* early" by her mother; in 1961 she made this entry in her journal: "Forgiveness and the eagerness *to protect*: these keep me from putting down the crudest shocks received from seven on. With my mother, my earliest instinct was to protect—to take care of, to endure. This, Dr. Wall once told me, is the instinct of a little boy. . . . Well, there it is. I *did* manage to become a woman. . . . Now, in my later years, I have no hatred or resentment left. But I still cannot describe some of the nightmares lived through, with love. So I shan't try to describe them at all. Finished. Over. . . . How do we survive such things? But it is long over. And forgiven . . ." [The last ellipses are Bogan's] (*JAMR*, 172).

The other love-hate force in Bogan's life was her Irishness. In an interview in *Partisan Review* on "The Situation in American Writing," she responded to the question about allegiance to class with a stern rebuke: "I did not know I was a member of a class until I was twenty-one; but I knew I was a member of a racial and religious minority, from an early age. . . . It was borne in upon me, all during my adolescence, that I was a 'Mick,' no matter what my other faults or virtues might be. It took me a long time to take this fact easily, and to understand the situation which gave rise to the minor persecutions I endured at the hands of supposedly educated and humane people" (*JAMR*, 52).

Arguably, Bogan's strong emphasis on control and order in her poetry grew out of her great aversion toward the unpredictability and chaos of her early emotional and domestic environment. Throughout her life she was impressed by examples of tidiness and efficiency, which she first experienced as a child during a stay with the Gardner family. Bogan writes recurringly and extensively in her journal, even from the distance of more than fifty years, of the nearly epiphanic impression made on her by Mrs. Gardner, a woman who seems to have been the exact antitype of Mary Bogan. What so awed the young Louise Bogan was the order of Mrs. Gardner's household, which remained inextricably linked in Bogan's mind to the absence of fear and vulnerability. "Order ran through the house. There were no bare spaces, or improvised nooks and corners; the kitchen shone with paint and oilcloth; the parlor, although miniscule, was a parlor through and through. . . . the meals were always on time. . . . And beyond the sitting room . . . ran Mrs. Gardner's workroom (she sewed), with a long bare table, a dress form, and a cabinet-like bureau where she kept her materials. This was the first workroom I had ever seen. I used to dream of it for years. . . . *One of everything* and everything ordered and complete. . . . Blessed order! Blessed thrift" (*JAMR*, 13–15). Seven years after this entry, Bogan turns again to the memory of Mrs. Gardner, picking up again the sewing image she had also used with her mother. Recalling how Mrs. Gardner had taught her to knot thread, she releases a rhetoric of praise. "Mrs. Gardner taught me to thread a needle and to put a knot at the end of my thumb. She rubbed the thread end between her right thumb and forefinger and the knot appeared. Bless her for the threaded needles and the knotted threads. Bless her for her jellies and preserves. . . . Bless her for the scrubbed pine table, and the clock on the mantel-shelf— . . . For her patchwork quilts and for the doll hiding the ball of string. . . . For her fringed linen towels on the towel racks. . . . No fear, no fear . . . [ellipses are Bogan's] No fear at Mrs. Gardner's!" (*JAMR*, 15–16).

Order, precision, and attention to form became ways of managing fear and disruption. The lesson of Mrs. Gardner emerges as an ethic for Bogan's poetry, just as the recurring sewing image—positively associated with Mrs. Gardner and a sign of the lack of pain when her mother is sewing—becomes an embedded image of Bogan as poet.

The emphasis of her art is on knotting, securing, making minutely and precisely a world of order and calm.

Bogan, however, was just a young girl when she escaped from the turbulence of her family life into a marriage she must have almost immediately regretted. In the December, 1917, issue of *Others*, along with "Betrothed" appeared a companion poem, "The Young Wife." This second poem, left out of *Body of This Death*, shows in explicit detail the painful death of a naïve, romantic attachment and in its place the beginnings of estrangement and resentment. The poem specifically addresses the disillusionment and betrayal felt by a sexually inexperienced girl at the easy knowledgeability of the male. Not only does she lose her feeling of uniqueness in the relationship, but her lover's previous partners have hardened into a perfected memory of sexuality and femininity that she, as a real woman, cannot equal.

Alexander died unexpectedly in 1920, but the couple had separated some time before that. Bogan, finding herself alone with a young child to support, did not return to her parents' home, but went to Boston to look for work. In a letter to Theodore Roethke in 1935, she succinctly captures the struggles of these years. "I had a child, from the age of 20, remember that, to hold me back, but I got up and went just the same, and I was, God help us, a woman. I took the first job that came along. And there was a depression on, as there is now, not quite so bad, but still pretty poor, and I lived on 18 bucks a week and spent a winter in a thin suit and muffler" (*WWL*, 98). She was also working through the guilt and loss of her husband's death. These emotions dominate the poems she was publishing in such journals as *Others*, *Poetry*, and increasingly, *The Measure*, with which she became associated in the early 1920s.[9] The legacy of this unfortunate early marriage and her subsequent struggle informs her first volume, *Body of This Death*, with its motif of broken, bitter relationships. She can even advocate a sacri-

9. The first issue of *The Measure* (New York) appeared in March, 1921, under the editorship of Frank Ernest Hill, with a revolving editorial core of such poets and critics as Maxwell Anderson, Genevieve Taggard, Louise Townsend Nicholl, and others. Bogan served as an editor from December, 1924, to February, 1925. The avowed preference of the group as set out by Anderson in the inaugural issue was for "musical and rounded forms" rather than the "half-said, half-conceived infantilities and whimsicalities of the dominant American school."

ficial celibacy in poems like "Ad Castitatem," "Knowledge," and "Men Loved Wholly Beyond Wisdom."

"Ad Castitatem" is a violent, extravagant poem renouncing sexuality by an admittedly sexual woman.

> I make the old sign.
> I invoke you,
> Chastity
> Life moves no more
> A breeze of flame.
>
> .   .   .   .   .   .
>
> I call upon you,
> who have not known you;
> I invoke you,
> Stranger though I be.

The Latin title, the ritual of invocation, and the gesture of the sign suggest the vows of the nun, as if Bogan is entering a celibate sisterhood in retreat from the destructive passions of the world. Underlying the poem is a strong sense of the speaker using a special kind of magic, availing herself of an ancient rite in order to ward off evil. The evil is human passion, which appears in the poem as a destroying flame that has "withered" nature indiscriminately and "ravaged" and "blackened" her own heart. The infertile landscape, the bitter tone, and imminent isolation are characteristic of Bogan, as is the resort to sacrificial measures in order to obtain control. In important ways, this poem is a companion to "Medusa." The personified figure of Chastity is Medusa in another guise, a variation on a type who appears under several names throughout Bogan's works. This figure is powerful, sometimes ominous, but essentially protective, and her force lies in her ability to arrest time and change. She is Medusa, Chastity, the Sleeping Fury, the interceding woman in "The Dream," becoming ultimately the force of poetry itself, representing the human-controlled frame in which time is stopped and process is formalized. From her early work on, Bogan returns to the lure of a powerful, mythic female who embodies inviolability, sanctuary, and control. Bogan liked to identify herself with strong women in history and myth. Replying to a scholar's query about her family origins, she said, "It is my firm belief that I was Messalina, the Woman of Andros . . . Boadicea, Mary Queen of Scots, Lucrezia Borgia, the feminine side of Leonardo . . . Saint Theresa of Avila." (*WWL*, 189).[10]

The passionate disavowals of "Ad Castitatem" are spent in the oriental mysticism of "Knowledge," where another prone speaker dedicates herself to a solitary, spiritual repose, suggestive of death. This figure is more fully revealed in "Portrait," in which the betrayed woman has moved beyond the painful reach of love and time, by physical or spiritual death, to a sterile landscape reminiscent of that in "A Tale."

> She has no need to fear the fall
> Of harvest from the laddered reach
> Of orchards, nor the tide gone ebbing
>   From the steep beach.

The title calls attention to her literal still life. The poem implies that when she was alive, the woman had "need to fear" the "ravage" brought by change and love. "Ravage" here echoes the threat in "Ad Castitatem," and like the speaker in the earlier poem, this woman could only survive by turning "stern and savage." Yet the quiet, elegiac tone of "Portrait" (a poem with curious parallels to Wordsworth's "A Slumber Did My Spirit Steal") suggests that only death brings the desired quittance of grief and alarm. Neither physical separation, chastity, nor stoic retreat have sufficed to ward off the "ravage" of being loved by men.

Yet, as elsewhere in *Body of This Death*, the impression lingers in "Portrait" that the "death" may be an outer pose disguising an inner, fiery life. Like the fixed, formalized surface of a painting, the woman has a certain flat presence with others; she is a glass on which they (presumably the men who love her) project their own conceptions, while her real life continues apart, out of reach.

This tension, this paradox between inner and outer selves, is a corollary of the physical and emotional isolation established in these poems, an isolation profoundly attributable to the difficulties per-

---

10. This statement was contained in a letter, apparently never sent, that responded to a research student who had sent her a lengthy questionnaire. The student's name is not given in *WWL* (189), but Ruth Limmer has informed me it was Stanley Kunitz.

ceived in feminine gender. It is the cry of the betrothed against the necessity that she sever the bonds of women to live with a stranger whose sexuality and presumption are repugnant to her; the vow of the speaker in "Ad Castitatem" is against the curse of sex as both threat and weapon. This isolation becomes startlingly objectified in the figure of the statue in one of Bogan's finest poems, "Statue and Birds." In this highly effective work, a marble girl stands at the heart of an empty winter arbor, the last human trace in a decaying formal scene. Her mind and exterior, like those of many Bogan personae, are grotesquely at odds. She is a type familiar from myth, a young girl transformed into a tree, a stone, or constellation to escape the violence of men or gods; her violation is prevented, but so, too, is her escape, and a panicked, vital consciousness lives on imprisoned.

The statue becomes literally the woman on a pedestal, a marble symbol for the conditions restricting all women. Thus the opening lines compare her to "the arrested wind," a free, natural force held in check. Similarly, the landscape surrounding her is largely artificial, where natural forces have been formalized and diverted. The leaves and vines have woven themselves into a pattern; the water is made to rise through the mechanical devices of a fountain; even the birds do not fly, but walk "closed up in their arrowy wings, / Dragging their sharp tails." The very mannered, restrained scene is designed to set off as the central feature the statue, which is paradoxically charged with an intensity of volition and gesture unmatched by anything around her. Her motion alone is violent. Her arms are "flung out in alarm / Or remonstrances," and "her heel is lifted,—she would flee,—." The punctuation of the last phrase emphasizes its sharpness and tension, building a sense of terror and desperation that is not fulfilled by the brief, muted closure: "the whistle of the birds / Fails on her breast." The descending sound of the phrase, the pause at *fails* when the reader expects *falls*, beautifully achieve the doom of hope and escape.

Symbolically, the marble girl represents women fixed by art as well as by artificiality, unable by definition—as statue, myth, pedestal, art—to express themselves. Inside the immobilizing form of marble, or sexual-social roles, such women are psychically and physically isolated. Even the statue's inner refusal, her gesture of alarm and remonstrance, ironically takes the shape of what the outside world sees as art or a pose. Because she is a statue, she cannot act or will; because she is a woman, she is trapped and isolated.

In poems following "Statue and Birds," the theme of the pain of gender intensifies. Paralysis and radical emotional denial impel the speaker of the well-known poem "Men Loved Wholly Beyond Wisdom." Here Bogan specifically resists the prodigal nature of women's love, so compulsive it burns like a fire in a thicket, totally consuming and destructive.

> Men loved wholly beyond wisdom
> Have the staff without the banner.
> Like a fire in a dry thicket
> Rising within women's eyes
> Is the love men must return.

Such love can be terrible in the homage it exacts, "the love men must return." Yet the alternative, to refuse to love at all, is equally grim, resulting in the emotional death of the woman.

> Heart, so subtle now, and trembling,
> What a marvel to be wise,
> To love never in this manner!
> To be quiet in the fern
> Like a thing gone dead and still,
> Listening to the prisoned cricket
> Shake its terrible, dissembling
> Music in the granite hill.

The image of the "prisoned cricket" exemplifies the irreducible feminine state, trapped and alone. Clearly, the sounds that come from her are "terrible" and "dissembling," rigidly controlled by the "granite hill" of personal and stylistic discipline.

"The Crows" continues the mood of self-disgust present in "Men Loved Wholly," while looking back to "Statue and Birds" for important corresponding images, most clearly in the winter setting and the dramatic use of birds.

> The woman who has grown old
> And knows desire must die,

> Yet turns to love again,
> Hears the crows' cry.

The speaker, like the statue, is trapped in a recalcitrant body while inwardly she teems with life and desire. Both the statue and this woman would flee their barren, withered world, but for the woman, turning again to love is made to appear as futile as the statue's lifted heel.

The collection's two central emotions—fear and denial—reach their nadir in the poem "Women." Whereas speakers in previous poems found it possible, even convincing, to place responsibility for isolation on forces such as tradition, magic, male figures, and age, the voice in "Women" internalizes the enemy and turns on her own feminine self. The "body of this death" becomes identified as her own female body. The poem's unrelieved bitterness toward gender epitomizes the worst kind of isolation, extending to encompass both the outward and inward worlds. Women are excoriated as stunted, constricted creatures, senselessly paralyzed and paralyzing.

> Women have no wilderness in them,
> They are provident instead,
> Content in the tight, hot cell of their hearts
> To eat dusty bread.

Hermetic, ingrown, they have sensuousness neither in themselves nor in their perception of the varied world about them.

> They do not see cattle cropping red winter grass,
> They do not hear
> Snow water going down under culverts
> Shallow and clear.

Everything they do evokes suffocation; life itself is a mistake for these eternally blundering women. Unable to build or create, they only destroy. Worse, they cannot even mother.

> They wait when they should turn to journeys,
> They stiffen when they should bend.
> They use against themselves that benevolence
> To which no man is friend.

> They hear in every whisper that speaks to them
> A shout and a cry.
> As like as not, when they take life over their door-sills
> They should let it go by.

The encompassing nature of the attack is clear from the bluntly inclusive title and the rapid, accusatory *They*'s with which half the lines
begin. The women are composite reductions of previous personae,
isolated from nature, the material world, productive social interchange
with either sex, and themselves.

Yet strangely enough, in many ways "Women" is tremendously freeing. Bogan herself always retained a particular fondness for the poem,
and later had it reissued privately. Unquestionably the poem is cathartic. In terms of the opening epigraph, it faces squarely and summarily
every aspect of gender that frustrates deliverance and admits death,
while it simultaneously abandons hope for a third-party rescue. Underlying its leaden charges is the awareness that only the self can alter the
self. Thus, it is fascinating in the context of the bitterness of "Women"
to read the poem Bogan placed immediately following it. "Last Hill in
a Vista" can be interpreted as an almost point-by-point reversal of the
indictments leveled in "Women." From the beginning lines it is as if,
miraculously, the women of the previous poem have escaped from
their "tight, hot cells" into the expansive landscape and freedom suggested in the title word "vista." Indeed the first word of each stanza is
the imperative "Come".

> Come, let us tell the weeds in ditches
> How we are poor, who once had riches,
> And lie out in the spare and sodden
> Pastures that the cows have trodden,
> The while an autumn night seals down
> The comforts of the wooden town.

The call "let us" is a radical break from the distancing of the cumula-
tive "they" in "Women," and marks only the third use of the inclusive
first-person plural in the twenty-one poems of the collection up to this
point; indeed, it is one of the rare expressions of fellowship with oth-

ers in all of Bogan's work. After poems of singularity and entrapment, this Fergus-like voice comes suddenly advocating a disregard of convention in favor of a journey under the stars. Throughout, the poem records an affinity to the natural world and its elements that was specifically denied women in the previous poem. The women in "Last Hill in a Vista" prefer the hills and fields to the "comforts of the wooden town," a phrase that suggests a limiting, negative propriety and domesticity, much like the subsequent "with stiff walls about us." These women risk cold and danger for a physical and psychic freedom. Their new condition makes their act courageous and determined, but the most crucial words are "we / Chose." The overriding trait of the previous speakers has been their lack of choice. They evince little control over the often horrific circumstances of their lives; the positive action here is revolutionary. Thus, the closure of "Last Hill in a Vista," unlike that normally characteristic of Bogan's poems, does not conclude or frustrate process but, rather, uniquely opens outward. The importance of this change in the sense of movement is seen by comparison with earlier poems, where stasis is structurally reinforced by an ambivalence in poetic closure that is a signature of *Body of This Death*. Repeatedly, the poems fail to achieve any sense of completion because of the alignment of phrases and images, which act to cancel each other out. This effect often occurs internally as well, revealing seeming alternatives of action only as means to the same end. This structural neutralization is a correlative of thematic immobility and futility. For example:

> Where something dreadful and another
> Look quietly upon each other.
> ("A Tale")

> The water will always fall, and will not fall
> And the tipped bell make no sound.
> ("Medusa")

> To escape is nothing, not to escape is nothing.
> ("A Letter")

> In fear of the rich mouth
> I kissed the thin,
> Even that was a trap

To snare me in.
("The Frightened Man")

Nothing was remembered, nothing forgotten
. . . .
Nothing was lost, nothing possessed.
("Words for Departure")

Alike upon the ground
Struck by the same withering
Lie the fruitful and the barren branch.
("Ad Castitatem")

Over what yields not, and what yields,
Alike in spring, and when there is only
Winter-burning in the fields.
("The Crows")

Their love is an eager meaninglessness,
Too tense or too lax.
("Women")

Unlike any poem preceding it in the volume, "Last Hill in a Vista" is the voice of rebellion and community, raised by women determined to free themselves mentally and physically from an oppressive environment. They have simply pulled up stakes and left, preferring the challenge of a risky liberty to the deceptive comfort and safety that diminishes their vitality and maturity. The remaining poems should be read in light of this change. For example, "Stanza," which was first published alongside "Last Hill in a Vista" in *Measure*, focuses on mythical women who were raped by men and who are now alone, going about their lives, refusing to be imprisoned in memory or trauma. Their attitude is one of self-sufficiency and specific indifference to the sexual impact of men on their lives. "Leda forgets the wings of the swan, / Danae has swept the gold away."

Similarly, "The Changed Woman" concerns a woman striving to live positively alone, which is a marked change from the behavior of earlier speakers. In it, "the cracked glass" suggests a split in the self, a duality existing in some prior state, while "wound" seems to be a familiar, negative metaphor for sexual experience. Both glass and wound are now "fused," "healed," and set "In the whole flesh." The male-female tension is emphasized in the third stanza by two patently phallic images and two female images—"Rocket and tree, and dome and bubble" —which are, to the speaker, images of treachery. Yet having "changed," the woman "need not trouble" with them any longer. The negative parts of her life belong to the past, while the fusing and healing belong to the present. The "unwise, heady / Dream" seems to be her desire to live independently, without the internal divisions brought on by insufficient sexual relationships. Here "unwise" registers a commendation, subverting as it does the desolation of wisdom in poems such as "Knowledge" and "Men Loved Wholly." Yet, the woman's life remains uneasy. Elsewhere the dream is "ever denied," and she fears she will "never . . . be forgiven" for her choice.

Following "The Changed Woman" is the curious "Chanson un peu naïve." The naïve, childish singer seems out of place beside the emerging, toughened women of the final poems. The style imitates the riddle songs of folk ballads, and the riddle in this case comes close to a parody of the volume's epigraph.

> What body can be ploughed,
> Sown, and broken yearly?
> She would not die, she vowed,
> But she has, nearly.

The answer to the riddle, the female body in childbirth, exemplifies broader discoveries the poems have been making about the vulnerabilities brought on by gender. The stanzas trace a girl's illusions about childbirth and love as she gradually answers the riddle but evades its implications. All that "flies free" at the end is her naïveté, and that is lost in cries. She undergoes no effective revelation; she is capable only of a "pretty boast" to conceal her bafflement and pain.

What emerges more subtly than the girl's plight, and what may explain the poem's placement at this stage, is the altered voice of the speaker. An undertone of mockery, amplified by the affected French title, the nursery rhyme meter and the pathetic rendering of the girl, measures the distance between this unenlightened figure and the more complex, initiated Bogan. Positively construed, the "chanson" is a mile-marker of the dominant voice's comparative security, flexibility, and even self-mockery. Yet the tone is still disturbing, for it hints of an unresolved disgust of gender that will continue to resurface in Bogan.

Body of This Death, however, closes out on the new upsurge of freedom and self-reliance. The penultimate poem of the volume, "Fifteenth Farewell," suggests by its title a move often attempted but never fully executed. The poem carries through the final break between a woman and her lover. The farewell seems necessitated by a relationship grown too prohibitive in personal cost. As the speaker explains, she regards the move as a matter of her own survival, fearing her selfhood will literally be buried under the man's domination. She refuses to comply with her psychic extinction, with covering "all that was" (her past life) with "all that will be" (her future with her lover).

> You may have all things from me, save my breath.
> The slight life in my throat will not give pause
> For your love, nor your loss, nor any cause.
> Shall I be made a panderer to death,
> Dig the green ground for darkness underneath,
> Let the dust serve me, covering all that was
> With all that will be?

She fully admits the loneliness that will attend her action, but she has redefined it; it is wrong to imagine loneliness as a physical setting, an absence of people, or any tangible emptiness. Rather, it is the unbridgeable separateness of an unequal human relationship: "Loneliness was the heart within your side." One can adjust to "simple, empty days" but not to the paralyzing alienation of "that chill / Resonant heart [striking] between my arms / Again." The poem closes in a mood and setting similar to "Last Hill in a Vista," with the first crucial steps having been taken but the consequences remaining untracked as darkness closes in.

> Now that I leave you, I shall be made lonely
> By simple empty days,—never that chill
> Resonant heart to strike between my arms
> Again, as though distraught for distance,—only
> Levels of evening, now, behind a hill,
> Or a late cock-crow from the darkening farms.

"Sonnet" deserves special attention as the concluding poem of *Body of This Death*. (It is also the only poem Bogan ever chose to have printed in italic, though this was dropped in subsequent printings.) Like "Last Hill in a Vista" and "Fifteenth Farewell," "Sonnet" is a poem of separation and independence; however, it turns more on the pain and uncertain future associated with independence.

> Since you would claim the sources of my thought
> Recall the meshes whence it sprang unlimed,
> The reedy traps which other hands have timed
> To close upon it. Conjure up the hot
> Blaze that it cleared so cleanly, or the snow
> Devised to strike it down. It will be free.
> Whatever nets draw in to prison me
> At length your eyes must turn to watch it go.
>
> My mouth, perhaps, may learn one thing too well,
> My body hear no echo save its own,
> Yet will the desperate mind, maddened and proud,
> Seek out the storm, escape the bitter spell
> That we obey, strain to the wind, be thrown
> Straight to its freedom in the thunderous cloud.

The poem focuses specifically on the entrapment of the mind, whereas the majority of previous poems have also focused on entrapment of the body. Here the will, the power of independent thought, drives the speaker to a "desperate" revolt against the "reedy traps" and "nets" of others, including, presumably, her lover. The distance traveled from the first poem of the volume, with its motive of escape, and this final poem is remarkable. The former is vague, third-person, and reactionary, motivated primarily by romantic escapism, while the latter is disciplined, courageous, first-person, and charged with a strong sense of self. The direction of deliverance moves figuratively from the earth / body toward the sky/spirit.

This orientation toward the last preserve of the self signals the emphasis of much of Bogan's subsequent work, yet the concluding sestet of "Sonnet" is a curious blend of the pride and madness of the pursuit. The liberation is seen in violent, reckless terms; danger is equal to triumph in the mingled sense of exhilaration and sacrificial release.

Behind Bogan's struggle is the specter of a solipsism that is potentially more enclosing than the isolation she seeks to escape. After *Body of This Death*, her fears, in very real ways, came true. She did "learn one thing too well," and her poetry often seems to have heard "no echo save its own." Her distrustful, cynical perspective, built on a reduction of the human and natural landscape, becomes habitual and predictable. The hope for freedom that the concluding poems of her first volume may imply solidifies in subsequent collections into profound isolation and suspicion. In *Dark Summer*, her second book, one comes upon the familiar stretches of barrenness set against fall, winter, night, and inclement days. The atmosphere of impending catastrophe is suggested by the volume's title. Modulations in theme and tone occur mostly in the new determination to survive and maintain rather than to solve or change.

This shift in emphasis is struck in the opening poem, whose title, "Winter Swan," parallels the oxymoronic title of the collection.

> It is a hollow garden, under the cloud;
> Beneath the heel a hollow earth is turned;
> Within the mind the live blood shouts aloud;
> Under the breast the willing blood is burned,
> Shut with the fire passed and the fire returned.
> But speak, you proud!
> Where lies the leaf-caught world once thought abiding,
> Now, but a dry disarray and artifice?
> Here, to the ripple cut by the cold, drifts this
> Bird, the long throat bent back, and the eyes in hiding.

Lacking other epigraphs, the book's overview could be taken from the first poem's concluding lines. The poem is a description of the artist— a beautiful, graceful figure surviving in a landscape leveled by winter, which it finds more congenial than the "artifice" of summer. What is important is the burning interior where "the live blood shouts" and that remains when the external world has receded. The final lines rhetorically answer the question, "Where lies the leaf-caught world once thought abiding." What survives is the artist, the isolated bird, who is able to exist in a cold, barren world where endurance depends on the fire within rather than on the mutable props of nature. The artist must successfully manage vulnerability—"The long throat bent back"—with hidden reserves of strength—"the eyes in hiding."

Throughout *Dark Summer* is a persistent sense of hiding; the self draws back from commitment and risk, while inwardly trying to consolidate its reserves in order to survive. The majority of poems attempt to respond to a terrible, yet frustratingly vague, vision that lies just beyond the bounds of the poem. Some poems try to forestall this vision—for example, "If We Take All Gold," "The Drum," and "Second Song"—while others, like "Didactic Piece," "Dark Summer," "Simple Autumnal," and "Late," try to lessen terror by anticipating the worst. Still others are retrospective; a feeling of aftershock underlies them, but the source of annihilation is never revealed, as in "The Cupola" "Feuer-nacht," "I Saw Eternity," and "Fiend's Weather." The poems of *Dark Summer* are, on the whole, more evasive than those of *Body of This Death*, and Bogan is more resolutely armored now than in any of the fine, early confessional poems such as "A Letter," "Words for Departure," "Survival," "The Young Wife," and the sequence "Beginning and End." But the quality of the isolation does not change, as seen, for example, in the poem "Cassandra." This poem, like the opening "Winter Swan," is a poem about the artist, in which Bogan is closer to herself as a woman poet and as a woman. Her choice of mythic figure comments on the essential anguish and futility with which she regarded both roles. Bogan expresses, besides the dilemma of any poet whose truths are ignored, the double curse of a speaker who is alienated as a poet and as a woman. Not only is there great pain in each creation, she cannot escape her own intensity and compulsion.

> To me, one silly task is like another.
> I bare the shambling tricks of lust and pride.
> This flesh will never give a child its mother,—
> Song, like a wing, tears through my breast, my side,
> And madness chooses out my voice again,
> Again. I am the chosen no hand saves:
> The shrieking heaven lifted over men,
> Not the dumb earth, wherein they set their graves.

The poem captures her sense of doom and necessity in the seemingly inevitable misunderstanding and hostility attendant upon her truths.

It touches, too, on Bogan's feeling that her poetry was unheeded, and even suggests her lack of a sense of community with other women. The insistence on "madness" in lines five and six, echoing the phrase "maddened and proud" from "Sonnet," is more than rhetorical, as Bogan experienced throughout her life periods of severe depression and was institutionalized at least three times for mental breakdowns.

Bogan gave up writing altogether after the publication of *Dark Summer*, citing her bitterness at "the continued reappearance of a personal legend that colored in the minds of many people who might be expected to be without bias, opinion of my work. . . . I abjured poetry. I no longer wished to say myself" (*WWL*, 56). On another occasion she stated, "I pronounce poetry a mug's game (I called it a gull's game for years) . . . I cannot and will not suffer for it any longer. With detachment and sanity I shall, in the future, observe; if to fall to the ground with my material makes me a madwoman, I abjure the trade" (*WWL*, 79). There were other reasons for Bogan's difficulty in writing. The 1930s were disruptive years for her. On Christmas Day, 1930, she lost all her possessions and her manuscripts in a fire that burned her home in Hillsdale, New York, to the ground. She had bought the home with Raymond Holden, her second husband, whom she married in July, 1925. In the early 1930s this marriage, too, had begun to break up, and she had problems with alcohol. At one point, Bogan claimed for herself the distinction of going "down in history as the heartiest female drinker among the female poets" (*WWL*, 144). In the spring of 1931, she was hospitalized for mental collapse. She wrote to her editor at Scribner's, "I refused to fall apart, so I have been taken apart, like a watch. I can truthfully say the fires of hell can hold no terrors for me now" (*WWL*, 57).

When she could write, it proved good therapy, as a letter to Allen Tate in October showed: "['Hypocrite Swift'] began as a literary exercise when I was in the country getting over what is popularly known as a nervous breakdown. . . . I suddenly realized that it was a poem, after all, and I lay my rapid recovery, from then on, to precisely that discovery" (*WWL*, 60). She wrote little, however, and her recovery was not going well. Closer to the truth was her letter early in 1932. "You cannot think what life with a shell resolves into. All this leaves little margin for creative effort" (*WWL*, 61). When she won a Guggenheim Travelling Fellowship in 1933, her situation seemed improved, but within nine months she had cut her trip short and had been hospitalized with a second, more severe collapse. Later, Bogan would describe herself as one "who had lain on the icy floor of the ninth circle of hell without speech and will and hope" (*WWL*, 99).

During the summer of 1935, Bogan had a brief, intense affair with Theodore Roethke, much her junior, that occasioned a "second blooming." But the more enduring situations were those that plagued her throughout her career—concern over money and her lack of audience. Finances were always tight; neither her poetry nor her work as a critic allowed her to live much above subsistence. Her letters are full of the precise sums she was paid for her work, often followed by an account of the necessities she spent them on.[11] She was reduced to asking, first, her editor at Scribner's, John Hall Wheelock, for money to send her daughter to school and, later, William Shawn, her boss at the *New Yorker*, for money to help pay her father's hospitalization bills. (She was paid $15 a week by the *New Yorker*.) Bogan even suffered the indignity of being evicted, though she lived in modest circumstances. (From 1937 to her death in 1970, she lived at the same address in Washington Heights, New York, alone after the early forties.)

When *The Sleeping Fury*, her third book of poetry, came out in 1937, her second marriage had long ended, she had survived two breakdowns, her position as poetry critic at the *New Yorker* was secure but taking all her time and energy, and she was forty years old. A retrospective of previous themes and a solidification of her style and direction, these twenty-five poems constitute her last book of entirely new work. Her three subsequent books—*Poems and New Poems* (1941), *Collected Poems* (1954), and *The Blue Estuaries* (1968)—each contain some new writing but are mainly collections of previously published poetry.

The Sleeping Fury turns firmly toward poetry as an acceptable means of handling the isolation repeatedly registered by the earlier volumes. Poetry presented the one inviolable extension of the self which allowed the control, reliability, and fulfillment impossible in human intimacy.

11. See, for example, Bogan's letter to Roethke, in which she explains how she spent the money she earned for "my great 'Baroque Comment' poem" (*WWL*, 107).

"Single Sonnet," "Henceforth from the Mind," and "Roman Fountain" demonstrate this shift in focus. Bogan could also be ironic about the poverty of such fulfillment, however, and takes a derisive tone in "Homunculus" toward the pretensions of her art. Except for the anomalous serenity of "Song for a Lyre," Bogan pairs poems of human connection with poems of disaffection, such as "Poem in Prose" with "Short Summary" and "Italian Morning" with "Man Alone." Unfortunately, her characteristic theme of disillusionment can also become an artificial pose, as in "To Wine," "At a Party," "Packet of Letters," and "Short Summary."

The title poem, the strongest of the collection, shows flashes of Bogan's former energy and courage in a rare expression of accommodation with her "fury," the intermittently recurring mythic female who is both muse and inner self, solace and threat. As such, the poem expresses the torment and the release of isolation. To understand the full meaning of the fury, it is necessary to examine what poetry, and the occasion of poetry writing, meant for Bogan. In an early essay, "The Springs of Poetry," she described the impulse to write.

> When [the poet] sets out to resolve, as rationally as he may, the tight irrational knot of his emotions, the poet hesitates for a moment. Unless the compulsion be absolute, as is rarely the case, the excitement of the resolution sets in only after this pause, filled with doubt and terror. He would choose anything, anything, rather than the desperate task before him: a book, music, talk, and laughter. Almost immediately the interruption is found, and the emotion diverted, or the poem is begun, and the desperation has its use. . . . Few poems are written in that special authentic rage because even a poet has a great many uses for grief and anger, beyond putting them into a poem. The poem is always a last resort.

Late in the essay, Bogan expresses several gifts she would bestow on a true poet. "He should be blessed by the power to write behind clenched teeth . . . blessed too, by a spirit as loud as a houseful of alien voices, ever tortured and divided with itself." She concludes with her conviction that poetry will always legitimately spring "from the passion of which every poet will always be afraid, but to which he should vow himself forever."[12]

These passages starkly reveal the mingled terror and release poetry held for Bogan; writing took place in the times of "last resort" when everything else had failed to "divert" her emotion. The poet is almost abused by the power of expression, or what she calls elsewhere in the essay "the maenad cry." She associates poetry with madness, particularly the madness of women—Cassandra, Medusa, maenads, the Sleeping Fury. But as Elaine Showalter (paraphrasing "madness hath its privileges") points out about insanity in women writers, it affords a tremendous power and freedom.[13] Bogan's description of the Fury captures the very essence of her conception of poetry.

You are here now,
Who were so loud and feared, in a symbol before me

. . . .

You who know what we love, but drive us to know it;
You with your whips and shrieks, bearer of truth and of solitude;
You who give, unlike men, to expiation your mercy.

Dropping the scourge when at last the scourged advances to meet it,
You, when the hunted turns, no longer remain the hunter
But stand silent and wait, at last returning his gaze.
("The Sleeping Fury")

The poet is "hunted" by the force of her vision, seeking to release the "anger and grief" in other means, until none avails but the rage of authentic poetry. Bogan's metaphor turns, in the moment of expression, to the paradox of the interchangeability of hunted and hunter. The appositive, "My scourge, my sister," suggests the extent to which she understands the muse, fury, and goddess as a deeply vitalizing but unreachable part of her self. Within the poem's frame the selves are at peace; the destructive division between them—destructive because of the pain engendered by poetry, the naked honesty of the self re-

12. Louise Bogan, "The Springs of Poetry," *New Republic*, December 5, 1923, Pt. II, p. 9.
13. Elaine Showalter, "Killing the Angel in the House: The Autonomy of Women Writers," *Antioch Review*, XXXII (1973), 344.

vealed—is, for the moment, overcome. But this is just a truce; the fury is only sleeping, only "for an hour quiet."

The terror returns in another extraordinary poem of her later writings, "The Dream."

O God, in the dream the terrible horse began
To paw at the air, and make for me with his blows.
Fear kept for thirty-five years poured through his mane,
And retribution equally old, or nearly, breathed through his nose.

Coward complete, I lay and wept on the ground
When some strong creature appeared, and leapt for the rein.
Another woman, as I lay half in a swound,
Leapt in the air, and clutched at the leather and chain.

Give him, she said, something of yours as a charm.
Throw him, she said, some poor thing you alone claim.
No, no, I cried, he hates me; he's out for harm,
And whether I yield or not, it is all the same.

But, like a lion in a legend, when I flung the glove
Pulled from my sweating, my cold right hand,
The terrible beast, that no one may understand,
Came to my side, and put down his head in love.

The sleeping fury of the one poem modulates to the more threatening dream of the other. Again the figure of a woman intercedes between the poet and annihilation. In view of other poems of this type and Bogan's knowledge of the classics, the destructive horse can be interpreted as representing Pegasus (offspring of Medusa) and the violent nature of poetry in Bogan's mind. Significantly, the horse is brought under control by two forces: the appearance of a strong woman, and the charm the speaker throws him. The strong woman represents her own power to control poetry, her inner strength, or both, while the charm—the glove from her right hand, her writing hand—represents in this dream world her bare-handed approach to poetry, the triumphing honesty and vision of her expression, which then appeases the "terrible horse." It is a clear variation on the hunted / hunter paradox of "The Sleeping Fury"; turning to face the nightmarish figure is the last resort that appeases it. Compare the final stanza of "The Dream" with the conclusion of "The Sleeping Fury":

> Beautiful now as a child whose hair, wet with rage and tears
> Clings to its face. And now I may look upon you,
> Having once met your eyes. You lie in sleep and forget me.
> Alone and strong in my peace, I look upon you in yours.

Women dominate these poems, as poet, victim, muse, and protector. It is surely Bogan's lifelong difficulties with gender that infuse her difficulties as a poet; but it is her inner strength as a woman that she is assured of and returns to. Thus "The Sleeping Fury" ends with Bogan as mythic mother, and the unicorn allusion ending "The Dream" casts her as queen and virgin. Each, however, is alone in her power and peace. It is clear, too, from Bogan's life and work that the separateness remained, while the calm was always short-lived. A later poem, "The Daemon," compresses in a short space the legacy of all her major statements on the muse and poet, showing little qualitative change from "Springs of Poetry" written years before.

> Must I tell again
> In the words I know
> For the ears of men
> The flesh, the blow?
>
> Must I show outright
> The bruise in the side,
> The halt in the night,
> And how death cried?
>
> Must I speak to the lot
> Who little bore?
> It said, *Why not?*
> It said, *Once more.*

The telling "Must I speak to the lot / Who little bore?" exemplifies her sense of isolation and singularity, while her failure to place her pain in a larger human context keeps any real magnanimity from her perspective.

Bogan's style was the direct expression of the extremity of emotion that she felt alone led to legitimate poetry. In her poetic, there was no room for meditative, exploratory vehicles; there is no sense of re-collecting in tranquillity. Rather, her poems were essential speech under the stress of the moment, creating what Marianne Moore called a "forged diction," wherein every thought and phrase is "compactness compacted." Poetry was to be infused only by large emotions, to avoid what Bogan termed "the small emotions with which poetry should not, and cannot deal." In her book, *The Advantage of Lyric*, Barbara Hardy defines *lyric* as simply "poetry [that] isolates feeling in small compass and so renders it at its most intense." Bogan's world did not admit change, and her lyric speech had the force of timelessness in its isolation from context, analyzation, and explanation. The formality of her expression was a function both of her need to control and her intent, as one critic has written, to "subordinat[e] her personality and experience to the discipline of strong language itself. . . . For Louise Bogan, the balance, measure, and above all the compressed simplicity of virtually all shorter lyric forms were synonymous not just with high artifice, but with clarity and integrity of attitude."[14] The extreme self-discipline and suppression that had enabled her emotionally and practically to survive a difficult girlhood, marital failures, mental break-downs, lifelong struggles with her muse and with her own nature, come out in a style pared to the bone of noun, verb, and preposition, the granite hill of form.

Bogan's tight style, barren images, bitter tone, and trapped personae remain characteristic of victimization: isolation brought on by the a priori curse of gender. Some of Bogan's poems, however, particularly among her later writings, express movement toward other stances. A few important poems move outward from the insular self to explore feminine isolation in the more external, social context of childhood and family experience found in personalization. For example, "Kept," develops the parallel between childhood toys and the adults we become, focusing on the image of a woman as doll; and

14. Marianne Moore, "Compactness Compacted," in Moore, *Predilections* (New York, 1955), 130; Louise Bogan, "July Dawn" (San Francisco, 1957). An insert to the folio contains a statement by Bogan on the poetic process; Barbara Hardy, *The Advantage of Lyric* (London, 1977), 1; Perlmutter, "A Doll's House," 167, 171.

"Heard by a Girl" records a young girl's socialization in the importance of surface beauty. Both poems turn on the ways women are taught to regard their bodies, and both note with great irony the alienation that results.

> . . . we at length begin
> To feel our nerves their strings,
> Their dust, our blood within.
>
> The dreadful painted bisque
> Becomes our very cheek.
> A doll's heart, faint at risk,
> Within our breast grows weak.
>
> Our hand the doll's, our tongue.
> ("Kept")

The speaker in "Heard by a Girl" concludes that the face is "The secret and the delicate mask."

In such poems as "Dark Summer," "The Sleeping Fury," and "Little Lobelia's Song," Bogan uses the image of the child, but she does not emphasize the child and her lyric form does not allow exploration of her memories. The glimpses remain oblique but fascinating. Interestingly, only when she steps out of her customary style to reflect the conversational rhythms and social concerns of W. H. Auden does she write her clearest personal commentary about women, in "Evening in the Sanitarium."

> The period of the wildest weeping, the fiercest delusion, is over.
> The women rest their tired half-healed hearts; they are almost well.
> Some of them will stay almost well always . . .
> .   .   .   .
> O fortunate bride, who never again will become elated after
>   childbirth!
> O lucky older wife, who has been cured of feeling unwanted!
> To the suburban railway station you will return, return,
> To meet forever Jim home on the 5:35.
> You will again be as normal and selfish and heartless as anybody else.

There is little left: the piano says it with its octave smile.
The soft carpets pad the thump and splinter of the suicide to be.
Everything will be splendid: the grandmother will not drink
    habitually.
The fruit salad will bloom on the plate like a bouquet
And the garden produce the blue-ribbon aquilegia.

The cats will be glad; the fathers feel justified; the mothers relieved.
The sons and husbands will no longer need to pay the bills.
Childhoods will be put away, the obscene nightmare abated.

The poem is a virtual catalogue of women trapped, abused, denied
their emotional and physical freedom, and condemned to pointless
lives in stultifying gender roles.

Several poems express characteristics of the split-self, often in connection with trapped personae. Thus, in poems like "Statue and Birds,"
"The Crows," and "Winter Swan," an inner self struggles with an outer
physical or social self. In these poems, the division is tense and unequal,
with one aspect of the personality being repudiated and unnatural. In
"The Crossed Apple," though, the two selves are an intentional compromise that the speaker has arranged between her sexual and spiritual desires. Her poems about mythic women and goddesses are split-
self poems in which her strong, artistic nature is projected as the
daemonic muse that compels her. Her nature and the muse achieve a
tenuous balance at the end of "The Sleeping Fury," but this accommodation is rare in Bogan. More often, one self must be rejected, and
there is little integration possible between them or the outside world.

Bogan approaches the positive separateness and self-affirmation of
validation perhaps only once, in the lovely valedictory, "After the Persian." Here isolation provides an alternative world, sharply distinct
from the style, images, and tone customary in her other writing.

The landscape is lush, fertile, and serene, the voice forgiving and
accepting of its fate; but as the first lines imply, this is achieved only at
the expense of denying her sources of poetry.

I do not wish to know
The depths of your terrible jungle:
From what nest your leopard leaps
Or what sterile lianas are at once your serpents' disguise and home.

> I am the dweller on the temperate threshold,
> The strip of corn and vine,
> Where all is translucence (the light!)
> Liquidity, and the sound of water.

She rejects the "terrible jungle" of the self; with the curious adjective "sterile," she rejects Medusa as her muse; and she announces her new landscape. Echoing images from scores of other poems, she condenses the pain of a sacrificial attitude toward life into the earned wisdom of these stately lines:

> I have wept with the spring storm;
> Burned with the brutal summer.
> Now, hearing the wind and the twanging bow-strings,
> I know what winter brings.
>
> . . . .
>
> All has been translated into treasure:
> Weightless as amber,
> Translucent as the currant on the branch,
> Dark as the rose's thorn.
>
> . . . .
>
> Goodbye, goodbye!
> There was so much to love, I could not love it all;
> I could not love it enough.
>
> Some things I overlooked, and some I could not find.
> Let the crystal clasp them
> When you drink your wine, in autumn.

The poem is beautiful, infused with a harmony almost unprecedented in Bogan, but it is a contrived resolution. The picture is static and the mood elegiac, achieved by a repression stated at the outset. Because of all she must deny to feel this peace, it is not really a poem of validation at all, but victimization in another guise.

More frequently, Louise Bogan creates barren, ominous landscapes that evoke a state of isolation in space and time. Her artistic fidelity is not so much to actual nature as it is to the inner world of the psyche, colored by emotional and psychological response. Subordination of the external to the service of an interior necessity also affects her depiction of personal relationships. There is little sense of interaction; hers is a poetry of aftermaths and summations, offering a minimum of context or circumstance.

The insularity of situation and response is an indication of the need to control, through her poetry, the literal and emotional aspects of her environments. Since the most capricious factor is the surging of nature, she negates nature and exerts her control over it by stylizing and transforming it in her work. Ironically, the result is not a Faustian or Adamic power but an even greater powerlessness and rigidity, dependent upon the denial of any nature and life that does not fit her frame. Tragically, what seems least to fit is the female body itself.

Bogan's stylistic and imagistic techniques consistently produce a highly didactic, single-mood poetry that obstructs a dialectic of counterpointing emotions and themes. What results is a poetry of no return. Isolating herself in a Clytemnestra-like stance against time, nature, humanity, and the cathartic release of emotion itself, Bogan's persona is a desperate, rigid figure. She has no recourse for escape except by appeal to the already victimized, insular self (her partial resolution in *Body of This Death*) or to the formality and control offered by poetry (her focus increasingly from *The Sleeping Fury* onward). The difficulty is that the poetic power on which the self relies dries up under the tremendous burden and the restriction in landscape and theme. This difficulty only intensifies the spiral of desperation and isolation that falls back on a shrinking poetic voice.

Recognition began to come to Bogan in the 1950s—honorary degrees, membership in the Academy of Arts and Letters, the Bollingen Prize in 1954 (for her *Collected Poems* which contained no new work)—but not during her creative years as a poet. She was again hospitalized for mental breakdown in the fall and winter of 1965. She had difficulty getting around at night and feared she was becoming senile: "I've forgotten large chunks of the multiplication tables, and have to count on my fingers" (*WWL*, 379). Troubles with alcohol returned; she was taking more and more Librium to get through the day; and her old struggle with writing continued to plague and distress her. In June, 1969, she wrote: "The struggle with *silence* still goes on. . . . Surely I can outwit this thing! I don't want to give up just yet" (*WWL*, 381). Seven months later she died alone in her apartment of what was diagnosed as a coronary occlusion.

The conditions of Louise Bogan's life and the perceptions of her poetry are perhaps best summed up by a letter she once wrote to May Sarton: "I have been *forced* to learn to wait, to be patient, to wait for the wheel to turn. . . . I have been *forced* to find a way of loving my destiny; of not opposing it too much with my will. I have been *forced* 'to forgive life' in order to get through existence at all. . . . My 'peace' and 'calm' are, as I have said again and again, too hard won to be lightly tossed aside."[15]

15. May Sarton, *A World of Light: Portraits and Celebrations* (New York, 1976), 227–28.

II / A Rescuer by Temperament
THE POETRY OF MAXINE KUMIN

A woman creeps on all fours through a squash patch in mid-September seeking out the late bloomers. . . . Frost is predicted for tonight. The woman will cover the tomatoes with an assortment of discarded bed-sheets and tablecloths, first setting out pans of water between the plants, for water acts in some perfectly logical way she does not understand to keep the temperature up. It is her annual aim to hold the fruit on the vines until October. Since they live near the top of a hill overlooking the river valley and her tomatoes grow on a south slope along the foundation stones of the house, it is not an unreasonable ambition. . . . She is a rescuer by temperament.
MAXINE KUMIN
"Wintering Over"

In a review of Maxine Kumin's second book, *The Privilege*, the critic and poet Robert Wallace was struck by her "vision of the isolation and enchantment of selfhood."[1] This impulse toward the mingled pleasures and terrors of a life lived psychically and physically alone drives her poetry. Her vision has changed in significant ways from the beginning of her poetic career to the present, with more terror in the early work and more acceptance and sympathy in the later. Much of the alteration stems from the gradual public and private reinforcement of her identity as a poet. When neither achievement as a poet nor satisfaction with the conventional woman's roles in her life offered a stable, reliable identity, her work was much bleaker in its statements, much darker in its voice. Assessing her life in an epistolary poem, "September 22," which concludes *The Privilege*, Kumin sums up the weariness and isolation that characterize her early work.

> I am tired of this history of loss!
> What drum can I beat to reach you?
> To be reasonable
> Is to put out the light.
> To be reasonable is to let go.

Generally speaking, Kumin's themes of isolation range from poems

1. Maxine Kumin, *The Privilege* (New York, 1965); Robert Wallace, "Down the Forked Hill Unsullied," *Poetry*, CVIII (1966), 121.

exhibiting characteristics of victimization similar to Louise Bogan's in their enclosure, passivity, fatalism, and resistance to nature, to poems that act as transitions between victimization and personalization, to poems in which the separately articulated stance of personalization fully emerges. While isolation through gender conflicts remains a primary concern, Kumin's conception of the source of isolation, as distinct from Bogan's, helps define the differences between each stance and suggests the changes Kumin's poetry goes through as it moves gradually from one stance to the other. In victimization, as demonstrated in the majority of Bogan's work, women are isolated a priori by the simple fact of being female. This accident of birth seems to trap them forever in a physical body and a set of emotions and behaviors that will inevitably result in their alienation and marginality. The sense of blind, unappeasable forces at work accounts for the frequent anger against nature as the realm that represents at once birth, physicality, and fate. Women can rail against their situation, but they cannot alter it. Personalization, however, while exhibiting the same concerns over gender conflicts and isolation, explores these in terms of a personal context, a nexus of events and persons that constitutes a woman's individual history. Above all, there is an attempt to see isolation as a process. Simone de Beauvoir captures the essential distinction in her statement, "One is not born a woman; one becomes a woman." Personalization articulates process, while victimization asserts finalities. To describe one stance as more hopeful than the other would be to disregard the continuing severity of the isolation each reveals; however, a greater potential for change, for flexibility, enters the voice now, along with a retention of personal power.

Maxine Kumin became a poet out of necessity. In the late 1950s she was in a state of desperation with her third pregnancy in five years; her closest friend had committed suicide in a postpartum depression; and her own choice appeared to be between art and breakdown. Her sanity was being threatened by the limitations of the life she was leading and by specific conflicts with conventional gender roles as wife, mother, and daughter.

I came to poetry as a way of saving myself because I was so wretchedly discontented and I felt so guilty about being discontented. It wasn't enough to be a housewife and mother. It didn't satisfy great chunks of me.[2]

When I was pregnant the third time I thought I was going to fall apart. It was long before the Women's Movement. There was nothing for me to identify with. I was unhappy and so guilty at myself for being unhappy, saying to myself, what is the matter with you that you are not enjoying this marvelous fulfillment, the fruit of your womb, et cetera, et cetera, and I started to write.[3]

Born Maxine Winokaur, June 6, 1925, in Philadelphia, and raised in a solidly middle-class environment, Kumin admits that marriage and motherhood had come to her simply as part of a life in which such things are the universally accepted schedule for women. "I was programmed into one kind of life, which was to say, get a college degree, get married, and have a family. . . . We did conform to the expectations of our generation—we married young and had children bang, bang, bang." Further, she was torn by a painful emotional deadlock with her mother that consumed her energies and identity. Her mother epitomized the traditional woman's role and strove to develop the traits of successful femininity in her daughter. Kumin, however, saw herself as plain and withdrawn, with masculine intellectual and athletic interests. Her greatest desire was to be an Olympic swimmer.

I was very much of a disappointment to my mother, she wanted me to be beautiful, radiant, a snazzy dresser, terribly popular. Instead of which I was an overweight, cross-eyed frump. For years and years and years. And rather withdrawn. What my very middle-class and striving parents wished for me was that I should make a successful marriage. There again I failed them because I married a poor man. . . . I was painfully estranged from my mother even through the early years of my marriage

2. Martha George Meek, "An Interview with Maxine Kumin," *Massachusetts Review* XVI (1975), 326.
3. Susan Allen Toth, "Fresh Air in the Garret: A Visit with Maxine Kumin," *Ms.*, (June, 1978), 37.

—it seemed there was nothing I could do that would please her.
I had to work that out in analysis.[4]

Kumin recalls, "I had been writing since I could hold a pencil," but
she was rebuffed in her early efforts by her creative writing teacher at
Radcliffe ("a very well-known American novelist . . . just a real smart
ass," who told her, "Say it with flowers, but for Christ's sake don't try to
write poems about it"). Consequently, it was not until much later, in
1957, when she joined a workshop led by John Holmes at the Boston
Center for Adult Education, that she took her first major step toward
assuming her identity as a poet. There she met another young housewife, Anne Sexton, who was also coming to poetry as a salvation for
difficulties brought on by deep-seated gender struggles. For the next
seventeen years, until Sexton's death in 1974, they were each other's
closest companion and critic, mutual sources of indispensable encour-
agement and support. Kumin writes of their relationship: "Anne and I
were inordinately close. We were more like sisters, I suppose; I never
had a sister. Somehow I think for both of us we filled so many of each
other's needs. . . . It was a rare day that we didn't see each other, and if
we didn't see each other we talked on the phone. . . . We frequently
would dial one another in the morning and stay connected all day . . .
and whistle into the phone when we wanted each other."[5] Sexton wrote
of Kumin, "Thank God for Maxine. She is close by always and knows
me. No one else who is within literal reach allows me to be real or
think."[6]

Through Holmes, whom Kumin calls her "Christian academic
daddy," she got a teaching job at Tufts. ("Because we were women . . .
we were deemed fit to teach only freshman composition to . . . dental
technicians.") In 1961, the Radcliffe Institute for Independent Study
appointed Sexton and Kumin as its first Scholars in Poetry. Kumin was
establishing herself but was still pulled back by misgivings about her
role: "I don't think I was a particularly good mother. When I first went
off to teach three days a week, I felt so guilty. When I think of all

4. Georgia Litwack, "A Conversation with Maxine Kumin, Poet," *Harvard Magazine*,
LXXIX (1977), 65, 68.
5. Toth, "Fresh Air," 37.
6. Anne Sexton, *A Self-Portrait in Letters*, eds. Linda Gray Sexton and Lois Ames
(Boston, 1977), 278.

the years I wasted on guilt. . . ."[7] Thus, it is necessary to understand Kumin's beginnings as a poet in a context of conflict over traditional female relationships, since it underlies the omnipresent sense of despair and pessimism in her first collections. In her later collections, the conflict provides her with one of her strongest voices and subjects. Recently she remarked: "I think the fact that women are coming out of the closet is one of the most positive things that's happened in this century. Maybe the only good thing in a fucked up world. I see immense changes in women's perceptions. . . . Now I have such a feeling of sisterhood. I find wherever I go I meet splendid women, and I'd a hell of a lot rather be with them."[8]

II

The feeling persists throughout *Halfway*, Kumin's first collection, and *The Privilege* that the poet is still finding her voice.[9] There is a certain amount of predictability and subject seeking in the lightweight, derivative satires and the occasional and seasonal poems, reflecting Kumin's beginning efforts as a poet writing magazine verse.[10] In addition, some of the poems express a generalized field of pain and bitterness scattered across a succession of landscapes and situations, not unlike Bogan's shifting environments in *Body of This Death*. Themes of death and powerlessness dominate, but again as in Bogan, the sources of crisis are oblique and fatalistic. *Halfway* divides into three sections whose signature phrases—"the nervous balance," "the incidence of time," "the effort of consent"—indicate concerns that run throughout Kumin's work. Each phrase suggests her interest in the most funda-

7. Toth, "Fresh Air," 37.
8. Elaine Showalter and Carol Smith, "A Nurturing Relationship: A Conversation with Anne Sexton and Maxine Kumin, April 15, 1974," *Women's Studies*, IV (1976), 132.
9. Maxine Kumin, *Halfway* (New York, 1961).
10. Acknowledging the fact that most of the poems in this volume preceded her better, more personal work, Kumin has said, "I look at that first book now . . . and there may be eight or ten out of the forty poems that I would keep, and the rest of them I would cheerfully shred." Toth, "Fresh Air," 37. Kumin recalls her first forays into trying to publish as a poet: "I bought a book called *Writing Light Verse and Prose Humor*, by Richard Armour, and I said, now if I don't publish anything by the time this baby is born, I'll give it up. And it didn't take any time at all. I sold a little four-line piece to the *Christian Science Monitor* for three dollars, which netted me a profit of fifty cents over the cost of the book, and I was off and running." Ibid.

mental questions of existence and the negative slant she gives them. Though Kumin is perhaps best known as a nature poet, even a pastoral poet, nature in her early books is ominous, often brutal, close in many ways to Bogan's world of "negligent death." Mice devour their litters, owls sound "like burned babies screaming," the benign summer lake drowns children, and spring's promise of renewal is empty and deceptive.

Perhaps because of the enormous turmoil and guilt over her discontent as wife, mother, and daughter, Kumin only occasionally deals specifically with this subject in her two early books; yet these poems are clearly among the strongest and most dramatically realized, suggesting her true subject. We can deduce from her personal situation and from the power of those poems which do address it that gender conflicts underlie her bleak outlook. Poems on this subject fall into both victimization and transitional stances.

"The First Rain of Spring" is an example of her oblique treatment of gender isolation. It is an early victimization poem in its imagery of enclosure, alienation from the body, resistance to nature, and the universalization of the estranging forces. The speaker meditates on the new growth of spring (represented by her children) that flourishes only at the expense of the old (herself). Her voice is one of great anguish, straining for objectivity against the compulsion for release. The irony of the renewing rain comes in her recognition, not only of her own mortality, but of her children's similar fate in the cycle. They sleep on innocently, unaware of how they are "closing the ring," which becomes the motif line of the poem. The primary image of the circle— repeated in the children's sleeping posture, the new spring seeds, the progress of the year, the speaker's helpless fist—is not a positive one; it clinches the final sense of dark, immutable forces enclosing life. Spring, rather than enhancing the speaker's existence, causes her to "store for death's fattening." As with Bogan's work, there is a strong stylistic tension in this poem between the flat account of surface fact and the strict use of rhyme and meter to keep the fierce emotion in check. The gender association is apparent in the speaker's bitter recognition of the pointlessness of her fertility, the surrender of her children to the mindless cycle.

Another victimization poem addresses Kumin's role as a daughter.

In "A Voice from the Roses," Kumin's identity as a poet and a woman struggles to be free of the inordinate dominance of her mother, pictured as the vengeful goddess Minerva of the Arachne myth. Minerva, goddess of the feminine accomplishments of spinning, weaving, and embroidery, represents the model by which Kumin fails. In the poem, however, Kumin asserts that her mother has mistaken her and has seen threats where there were none.

> Having confused me
> with the nearest of her nine
> nimble sisters—
> the beautiful one
> she witched into seizures
> of drools and tremors
> for picking away at her needlepoint—
> my mother directed the craft
> of her vengeance against me.

As a result, the daughter has spent her life attempting to prove to her mother (and to herself) who she really is, and thus to end the curse. In the myth, Minerva, enraged at Arachne's challenge to the goddess' superiority in her arts, defeats her in fierce competition. When the girl hangs herself out of humiliation, the goddess transforms her into a spider; in this way, she can continue to weave, but she cannot threaten Minerva. In Kumin's version of the myth, she is not Arachne, and she has not challenged the mother/goddess. Nevertheless, she has been changed into a spider, that is, a person of low self-esteem and powerlessness, whose only means of reaching the mother are through intricate weavings. These weavings represent her poetry, a system of elaborate encodings that are disguised rebellions against the overwhelming influence of her mother.

> I have lain
> on this thorn thirty years
> spinning out of my
> pear-shaped belly
> my puffball pearl-gray belly
> always perfectly damp,

intricate maps of my brainpan,
lines and ligatures
that catch the morning light
and carve it into prisms;
you might say, messages.

Nevertheless
it is rooted. It is
raising a tree inside me.
The buds of my mother's arbor
grow ripe in my sex.
Mother, Queen of the roses,
wearer of forks and petals,
when may I be free of you?
When will I be done
with the force of your magic?

These messages, her poems, have scattered their force through for-
malities and prisms whose beauty and lightness disguise the belly and
guts and pain behind them. Thus, with no literal or symbolic way of
exorcising the thorn, the daughter has internalized it until it has become an entire tree. The poem reveals a daughter emotionally isolated
from her mother, a contradictory figure who extorts a set of behaviors
at the same time she punishes any challenge they might raise. Moreover, the daughter is isolated from her own intellectual power and her
physical body, taught to regard each as repulsive. The spidery, doubt-
ridden daughter spins complicated graphs of her self to reach the
mother and to establish her identity, but fails at each task because she
cannot come out from under the power of the mother/Goddess/Queen.
She is thereby kept from fulfilling herself as a woman and poet.

"A Voice from the Roses" uses several techniques to put the pain
and immediacy of Kumin's experience at a distance—the intermediary
myth, the accumulation of references to poetry without mentioning it
precisely ("lines," "maps," "prisms"), and the syntactical postponement
of stating the real problem, which is given with a buffering qualification, "you might say, messages." This distancing, the alienation from
the body, the imagery of enclosure, the internalization of anger, are all
characteristics of a classic victimization poem.

When addressing her relationship to her father, for instance in "The Marauder" and "A Hundred Nights," Kumin moves closer to personalization, no doubt because this relationship was less painful, required fewer self-protective devices, and involved less awareness of her own diminishment and powerlessness. Her approach to these poems, which share with "A Voice from the Roses" her conflicts as a daughter, provides a good indication of the different emphases in victimization and personalization. In "A Hundred Nights," the child-speaker wakes to find bats loose near her bed, only to be further terrified by her father and her uncles, who rush in with rug beaters to protect her. The bat, "the terrible mouse with wings / notched like bread knives," is no more repulsive than the precipitous violence and chaos of the invading male figures: "Father in his union suit / came a hundred sultry nights, / came like an avenging ghost." So powerful is this memory that she has magnified its occurrence to a "hundred nights" in her imagination, claiming in the final lines:

> No matter that my parents say
> it only happened twice that way
>
> and all the rest are in my head.
> Once before my father dies,
> I mean to ask him why he chose
> to loose those furies at my bed.

The father is thus held responsible for the daughter's loss of peace and innocence. By the poem's end, both the bats, "those flapping rats," and the father seem to be in league against the child. Although she begs him to kill them, to remove her fears and guilts, he merely stuns the bats and frees them at the window. He therefore fails his daughter, augments her fears, and aligns himself with the invading, threatening forces in her bedroom. Her description of the bats as "the heave of wings come down horn-mad / to thump and thwack against the shade," parallels her perception of the father waving the rug beater "like an avenging ghost" and the uncles, who "ran down / a hundred nights to cheer and groan / as Father swore and chipped the plaster."

This theme of paternal violence returns in "The Marauder," with the father's zealous intention to keep his child safe from kidnapping.

Instead, she becomes obsessed with thoughts of her own death and re-
pulsiveness. He erects what amounts to a literal and psychic cage
around her, inducing a siege of fear and guilt.

> . . . you came to fill
> my windows up with wire
> and fastened me into your fear;
> and we had ropes in case of fire.
> You had a Luger pistol, left, I think
> . . . I was the prize and prisoner
> sealed in at bedtime, counting each steel link.
>
> . . . I tell you, ever since,
> these taints of violence
> sit in my chest like a sixth sense,
> an aura of death I cannot shrug off.
>
> Father, who kept me safe
> and put the demons in my house,
> and built up your sure creed inside my bones. . . .

Through his custodial efforts to preserve his "prize and prisoner," he
becomes "The Marauder" of the title, the ironic instrument of his
daughter's fears of rape and death. Although these poems still register
a degree of alienation from the body, entrapment, and internalization,
the speaker is not a victim as she is in "A Voice from the Roses." The
attitude is crucially distinct and the style is altered. The stronger narrative line depends on the realistic evocation of an actual event rather
than on the prop of myth. The exemplification through detail involves
a progressive discovery and revelation that is more personal finally
than the summary telling of Kumin's poem to her mother.

The conscious distancing in "A Voice from the Roses" does not figure in the poems to her father. Further, these poems describe situations the speaker has to some extent moved beyond, so that the enclosure motif is not as determining or final. Her rebellious tone is a
sign of her growing control.

Kumin moves from isolation as a daughter to isolation in her roles
as wife and mother in the very effective personalization poem "The

Appointment." The speaker's demanding inner self takes the form of a wolf who stands at the foot of her bed (the bed symbolizes what defines and confines a woman's role). Like the tree in "A Voice from the Roses," the wolf has become so much a part of her that she hardly starts at his presence, yet both symbols represent significant parts of herself that occur completely alone. The wolf does not watch the house, the children, or the husband, and by implication it does not address the speaker in her roles as housewife, mother, or lover. The wolf is another self that she tries to deny: "I lie to him nightlong. / I delay him with praises." Since no one else can see the wolf, no one sees the part of the speaker he symbolizes. The wolf is both familiar to the woman ("In the morning we wash / together chummily") and frightening because of the threat it offers to her other roles. The speaker believes she cannot accommodate both the wolf of selfhood and her traditional gender roles. The impending crisis of the situation looms in the tension embedded in the images of her environment: "the hot fog" is "fingering the window locks"; "the daffodils / wait in the wings / like spearholders"; the children are "fisted" in dreams; and she thinks of her husband as having been "fixed over me / all these good years." These subtly ominous images, together with the wolf, capture the destructive potential of the situation, but there is still room for resolution. The woman retains meaningful ties to both worlds. Her status remains ambivalent, but not finalized.

Not surprisingly, Kumin finds a special attraction in figures whose solitariness is part of a personal strength and choice, for example, Isabella Gardner, and the high diver and the competitive swimmer. In addition, tributes to Thoreau appear in both *Halfway* and *The Privilege*, whereas subsequent collections develop the personae of Henry Manley, a New England farmer, and the mythical Hermit as emblematic loners whose isolation is fruitful and positive along the lines of validation. Kumin's own isolation from nature, from others, and from her roles as woman creates a milieu of personal tension. Poems in her early work that genuinely perceive joy in the present are very rare. Instead, she writes "wish poems," which shift into, or are written entirely in, the imperative or subjunctive moods and in which intimacy and happiness are envisioned as existing elsewhere. An example is "A Verse Against Winter," fittingly titled as a ritual invocation against loss.

Ere dust sift in my mouth
and pennies quench my eyes,
and pines enwrap my thighs
and roots invade my south;

.   .   .   .

let love be in my house

.   .   .   .

Let death that angry mouse,
come scratch behind my head.
Time spangle in my bed;
Now love, be in my house.

Kumin's similarity to Bogan stands out especially in her early work. Both are concerned with the sterility of relationships, the lack of renewal in natural or human life, the attraction of the solitary, the absence of joy save in wishful dreams (though Kumin is able to fantasize to a degree that Bogan is not), and the central powerlessness of the speaker. Moreover, their styles are similar in the extent to which both poets employ formal techniques to control the emotions behind the poetry and to act as permission for the emotion. Kumin has said, "I have to be pretty comfortable with what I'm writing to write a free-verse poem; or else not terribly, deeply involved. I almost always put some sort of formal stricture on a deeply-felt poem, maybe not rhyme, but at least a stanzaic pattern." Referring to a very personal poem about her father, she adds, "I wrote that elegy 'The Pawnbroker,' believe it or not, in syllabics as well as rhyme. That's how terrified I was of writing it." [11] For Bogan as well, the rigidity of technique made the extreme of her emotion legitimate and acceptable. Although Kumin is not nearly the strict formalist Bogan is, nearly half of the poems in *Halfway* and *The Privilege* depend on rhyme.

The state of Kumin's life when she was establishing herself as a poet bespeaks difficulties and tensions that do not find their way into the poems of this period. Kumin has noted, on several occasions, her affinity for Marianne Moore's dictum to be "as clear as natural reticence will allow you to be." Yet her early volumes are neither wholly clear nor natural. Too often, situations are conventional and derivative, the

11. Meek, "An Interview," 322.

voice self-protected and distant. The persistent sense of deep hurt and alienation is seldom centered or focused. When it is, powerful, effective poems result, but she is still finding her stride as a poet. The poems of *Halfway* and *The Privilege* are closest in feeling to the isolation and victimization of Bogan in their lack of renewal, their powerlessness, repression, and images of enclosure and barrenness.

Two crucial factors in Kumin's life helped change her perspective over this period of apprenticeship: her increasing recognition as a poet through grants, prizes, and publication, and a prolonged period of analysis. Kumin asserts that "analysis opened me to so many possibilities. . . . It was immensely helpful. I was having a very bad time. My father was dying. I was having a lot of problems—with that, with my position in the family, with my mother, all the rest of it. . . . All I knew was I had to get rid of the terrible anxiety or I would die of it—it felt that bad." [12] Thus, Kumin begins to move away from her stance of victimization and turn toward personalization poems, exploring familial connections and her relations as wife, mother, daughter and, now, poet. A sense of context and causality about gender increasingly replaces the previous notion of blind fate and inscrutable forces. In particular, the natural landscape becomes less threatening, while simultaneously she is more accepting of her own physical self. She can admit the center of her grief and pain in the human nexus, and no longer needs to project emotional sterility and isolation on nature. Indeed, nature grows in its ability to compensate her for her human isolation, and it provides a milieu within which she can assert and test her inner resilience and self-sufficiency.

III

In *The Nightmare Factory*, published in 1970, Kumin moves firmly to personalization, finding her strength as a poet in the themes that stood out, but did not fully emerge, in her previous work. [13] She shows new willingness to speak in her role as lover and wife and to explore with more depth and subtlety the past and present constellations of her family. Kumin agrees with this assessment, adding, "Somehow as I get

12. Litwack, "A Conversation," 68.
13. Maxine Kumin, *The Nightmare Factory* (New York, 1970).

older I feel freer to deal with material that I might have shied away from ten or fifteen years ago. Also we must take into account changing social attitudes attributable at least in part to the Women's Movement."[14] *The Nightmare Factory* contains individual sections entirely on sexual and familial subjects—"For Such a Man and Woman" and "The Tribal Poems." Nature, too, building on the brief "Joppa Diary" section in *The Privilege*, becomes particularized as the New England locale, coincident with the emerging importance in Kumin's personal life of her farm in New Hampshire. The rural area becomes a permanent environmental and symbolic feature of her writing. She writes with more romanticism about the land and its creatures than she has before, and shows a growing sense of independence and inner strength from subduing the practical struggles of living in so remote and primitive a manner. Her way of life provides moments of vision and peace that seemed earlier to be denied her, though these moments are still rendered primarily in the style of wish poems. The presence of death is not diminished, but the speaker is able to deal more effectively with specific griefs—the death of her mare, the slaughter of calves, the departure of her children, the fears of her own illness—than with the amorphous phantom of "a history of loss."

In *House, Bridge, Fountain, Gate* (1975) and *The Retrieval System* (1978), she continues to move even further toward a complex and mature understanding of her isolation as a woman.[15] In a wise and compassionate voice she expands themes already evident but often subordinated in the early work: the traumas of childhood, the difficulties with her mother, cultural rituals that work to estrange women from men, from other women, and from their own needs. Against these difficulties, she chooses a physical retreat, a literal reclusiveness in which the land and the concentration of her own physical and artistic labors provide a measure of protection against the margin of loss. It is the bedrock of strength and empathy in her voice that characterizes personalization, though a few poems of victimization still appear in Kumin. More typically, her perspective is that of a woman who is profoundly affected by disaffection and the wastage of human potential, but who fights against retreating into bitterness or resignation.

14. Kumin to the author, December 1, 1978.
15. Maxine Kumin, *House, Bridge, Fountain, Gate* (New York, 1975); *The Retrieval System* (New York, 1978).

Personalization is a stance of exploration, a personal probing of isolation in which one's existence and one's discoveries are not foregone conclusions, as they are in victimization poems. The speaker shows more flexibility and power. The number of Kumin's poems specifically probing her experience as a wife and mother increases markedly in *The Nightmare Factory*. The effect of gender roles on sexual divisions is explored in the poem "A Family Man," in which the speaker is in bed with a man who shows her photographs from his wallet. The couple's conflicting reactions to the pictures exemplify their basic emotional and sexual differentiation.

> Out of the celluloid album, cleverly as a shill
> you pull an old snap of yourself squatting beside
> a stag you shot early in the war in the Black Hills.
> The dog tags dangle on your naked chest.
> The rifle, broken, lies across your knees.
> What do I say to the killer you love best,
> that boy-man full of his summer expertise?

The man clearly prides himself on this emblematic masculinity in the pose of "killer." Both the hunt and the war seem a kind of summer excursion full of invigorating expertise. To the woman, the picture's fusion of brutality and pleasure represents a uniquely male amalgam of death and desire. To the man, the iconographic photo he carries in his wallet represents the part of himself he loves. The fact that the poem is set amidst a sexual encounter suggests the operation of these factors in determining the nature of their intimacy. The woman feels the man can only relate to her with the objectification and insensitivity revealed in the photo. Once she has associated him with this repugnant male destructiveness, she has nothing to say to him or the estranging image he leaves.

> What can I say to the killer you love best?
> . . . .
> I with no place in the file will
> wake on dark mornings alone with him in my head.

Two points of irony emerge in the poem: the title, "A Family Man," which contrasts the man's respectable, suburban exterior with the dark self he is in his heart; and the phrase, "talking in bed," which provides the poem's cynical frame. The phrase refers to an admirable attempt to get beyond strictly sexual ways of relating, but the result only exposes their split over basic conceptions of self, and the speaker ends registering her isolation.

In the poem "After Love," Kumin returns to the image of the wolf she used in "The Appointment" to symbolize the fears and voraciousness of her isolation ("This is my wolf"). "After Love" follows two poems that evoke the sensuous transformation of sex—"We Are" and "Together." The title and the poem's placement in the text seem designed to stress the poet's sense of how even positive intimacy is eclipsed in the inevitable return to a more durable psychic separation.

> Afterwards, the compromise.
> Bodies resume their boundaries.
>
> These legs, for instance, mine.
> Your arms take you back in.
>
> Spoons of our fingers, lips
> admit their ownership.
>
> The bedding yawns, a door
> blows aimlessly ajar
>
> and overhead, a plane
> singsongs coming down.
>
> Nothing is changed, except
> there was a moment when
>
> the wolf, the mongering wolf
> who stands outside the self
>
> lay lightly down and slept.

The perspective is resigned to the conclusion that "nothing is changed." Physically the lovers withdraw into themselves, articulating "boundaries" and "ownership" that correspond to emotional and experiential demarcations. The poem builds on images of emptiness—the banging door, the plane that may be landing or falling, the bedding that yawns (implying both the boredom and the gulf in their relationship). Briefly during the sexual act their separateness is allayed, the wolf lies down, but in the aftermath their essentially isolated identities are reasserted. Important distinctions, though, make this a poem of personalization rather than victimization. The speaker is not eclipsed or trapped by the encounter—it is a "compromise." Both the man and the woman, though estranged at the end, are equally present or negligible in the situation. In addition, the wolf has lost some of its exclusive association with the speaker, appearing as *the* wolf, rather than *my* wolf as it had in "The Appointment." Finally, the nervous edge, the rigidity in the voice or situation so frequently found in poems of victimization, is missing.

By contrast, "The Masochist" is a victimization poem written, interestingly enough, in a style more typical of Anne Sexton than of Kumin. The speaker has been physically and emotionally exploited by a vindictive male figure who has broken her back in a conventional gesture of power.

> My black-eyed lover broke my back,
> that hinge I swung on in and out
> and never once thought twice about,
>
> expecting a life-time guarantee.
> He snapped that simple hinge for me.
> My black-eyed lover broke my back.
>
> All delicate with touch and praise
> he one by one undid the screws
> that held the pin inside the cup
>
> and when I toppled like a door
> —his bitch, his bountiful, his whore—
> he did not stay to lift me up.

But the poem clearly lacks the subtlety of insight, the specificity of emotion and situation that is Kumin's strength, indicating that at this point in her writing, such a poem and perspective constitute more of an exercise than an authentic expression of a stance.

Another group of poems from *The Nightmare Factory* explores isolation between mothers and daughters, again in ways characteristic of personalization. The most interesting of these poems is "The Fairest One of All," which takes its frame from a fairy tale. The underlying legend is "Snow White"; the daughter is cast as "the fairest," while the poet is the vengeful mother. The poem opens with the mother's imaginative vision of what "ought to befall" her daughter. She sees her as a beautiful ballerina, the central figure of a magical setting.

> Pirouettes of you are in order.
> There ought to be slithers of satin
> and diamonds buckled to your ears . . .
>   A series of mirrors
> ought to repeat your bare shoulders
> while someone quite gravely
> sprinkles rosin on the parquet floor
> and the orchestra adjusts itself
> to the violin's clear A.
>
> .   .   .   .
> All this ought to befall.

The reality, however, is quite different; the daughter stands at the ironing board,

> . . . slicking
> one seam from wrist to shoulder
> parting nine pleats with the hot metal nose
> and closing them crisp as a lettuce cup
>
> .   .   .   .
> with hands that kiss, smack, fold, tuck.

The vision of the daughter as a ballerina gave her a power, grace, and pride that seem prodigally wasted on her efficiency as she irons, no matter how lovely she may look doing it.

The poem shifts again into the mother's imagination, with the two women more clearly cast in the roles of Snow White and the step-mother. The poem draws on the folktale's ritual of enmity between mother and daughter, and the subsequent alliance of the daughter with the male huntsman to defeat the mother. The initial beautiful wish for her daughter to be a lovely, powerful solitary dissolves under the mother's sense of the worst.

> . . . let there be
> no mistaking how that dark scheme runs.
> Too soon all this will befall.

> Too soon the huntsman will come.
> He will bring me the heart of a wild boar
> and I in error will have it salted and cooked
> and I in malice will eat it bit by bit
> thinking it yours.
> And as we both know, at the appropriate moment
> I will be consumed by an inexorable fire
> as you look on.

The speaker apprehends an estrangement that will pit daughter against mother, with each struggling to survive through the destruction of the other. At the center of the conflict is their competition for the male. This conflict is shown in the fairy tale in the stepmother's desperate need to remain beautiful, and her subsequent revenge when her daughter eclipses her as "the fairest one of all." Despite the "dark scheme," the speaker dreams of another outcome for her daughter which allows the girl independence and possible maintenance of her bond with the mother. It is uncertain whether she has the power to communicate this to her daughter, much less to realize it.

As in "A Voice from the Roses," Kumin turns to a preexisting thematic structure for "The Fairest One of All." Unlike in the earlier poem, Kumin alternates the mythic parts with precise, colloquial images of the real daughter in an ordinary setting. The daughter is not fully enclosed by the framing tale, and the other participants are not stock, generalized figures. There is an empathetic understanding of both the mother's and the daughter's roles that is entirely missing in "A Voice from the Roses," and at least during the time frame of the poem, the two women are still allied. Further, the speaker struggles against the vision of estrangement, clearly loving her daughter, unlike the uncompromising Minerva-mother portrayed in "A Voice from the Roses." The speaker's guilt also diminishes the sense of victimization, though the outcome of the poem remains troubled and bleak.

In 1973, Maxine Kumin won the Pulitzer Prize for her book *Up Country: Poems of New England, New and Selected*.[16] The collection is divided into four sections, the first consisting of new work. The opening

16. Maxine Kumin, *Up Country: Poems of New England, New and Selected* (New York, 1972). Kumin credits Anne Sexton for titling this book and in turn claims that she gave the title to Sexton's *Transformations*.

eight poems, nearly half the new writing, develop a new Kumin persona in the mythical character of the Hermit. The Hermit is very much in the mold of an idealized Thoreau, whom Kumin had used twice previously to represent a positive isolation, but never to the extent to which she now uses the Hermit. His positivity and self-sufficiency represent a marked advance over her earlier accounts of isolation. Two aspects of her new sense of isolation are noteworthy: first, Kumin turns to a male persona rather than projecting herself in this role; second, physical isolation becomes a positive force, linked to the growing value of simple, physical nature. Visible in only a few early poems—"Morning Swim," "My Quotable Friend," "The Habits of Childhood," "Riding in the Rain"—nature comes into its own in *Up Country* as the realm of sustenance, continuity, and reliability that Kumin cannot find among her own kind. She is able to discover in the land an identity that nature does not diminish in the way the emotional and sexual divisions of the world do. The highest expression of the ideal life—solitary, self-sufficient, and in harmony with nature—occurs in the Hermit poems rather than in her first-person poems.

The Hermit poems, which open the collection, appear to be thematically paired with the opening poems of the second section, taken from *The Nightmare Factory*. This arrangement enhances the appeal of the Hermit's world by contrasting it with the human flaws of Kumin's world. The pairing is also a study in positive isolation, such as that found in validation, wherein the speaker's singularity results in an alternative world. The contrasts also reveal Kumin's ambivalence in her sense of isolation: she is able to project a healthy, desirable singleness on the male Hermit, but she cannot realize it on her own female terms. Thus in "The Hermit Wakes to Bird Sounds," he begins his morning contentedly, hearing the cacaphony that is "endearing," a "staccato rush," "a promise of water," from "all the machines of morning." But Kumin, in "Whippoorwill," hears the birds in a melancholy night setting and thinks:

> . . . Such shabbiness
> in those three clear tones!
> Pinched lips, missed chances,
> runaways, loves you treated badly,

> a room full of discards,
> I among them.

In "The Hermit Meets the Skunk," the Hermit reacts to death practically and unsentimentally; it is foul and unpleasant, but also necessary and desirable: "the mother bed, the ripe taste / of carrion, the green kiss." This approach to death is paired with Kumin's, in "For a Shetland Pony Brood Mare Who Died in Her Barren Year," in which the speaker has much difficulty adjusting to the spectacle of her old horse dying of a false pregnancy. Rather than a new foal, it is the ghost of her own death the mare carries. The speaker is aghast at the false renewal, the swelled milk bag, the whole "obstinate machine" of gestation, and also of death. Other paired views of life and death are "The Hermit Picks Berries" and "The Vealers," and "The Hermit Goes Up Attic" and "Cellar Hole in Joppa."

The Hermit series concludes with the strongest poem of self-sufficiency, "The Hermit Reviews His Simples." In the arcane lore of the land, in the proverbs and poultices of the past, the Hermit "reviews" the foundation of his organic view of existence and the mainstay of his isolation. In the plants and in his personal sense of peace, he has all he needs for sustenance.

> But the hermit does not sicken.
> He has put his June wine in the cupboard.
> He has laid down the handbook of simples.
> He calls the old dog from the front stoop
> and goes on walking his fences.

This figure not only triumphs rather invigoratingly over emotional and physical solitude, but he depends on it. Kumin praised him, trying to approximate his ideal in her life-style on her farm in rural New Hampshire. She remains torn, however, by the difficulties of the human ties the Hermit is able to evade. The Hermit is a valuable wish projection, but he cannot answer her unresolved problems with gender roles past and present. These she continues to explore in *House, Bridge, Fountain, Gate* and her much-acclaimed *The Retrieval System*.

House, Bridge, Fountain, Gate, Kumin's fifth book of poems, carries a dedication to Anne Sexton, who died the year the book was published.

Though it is not until several years later, in *The Retrieval System*, that Kumin is able to address this loss directly in her writing, the poems in this collection speak about the female experience with increasing honesty, which itself seems a tribute to Sexton. There is a growing confidence and precision in her handling of environments and relationships. In particular, her understanding of mothers, daughters, and families expands and matures. In the opening poem of the volume, "History Lesson," Kumin reveals a desire for the miraculous transmutation of her life into a unique connection to female heritage and lore. The "history lesson" is the mother's recounting to her daughter of the child's early years of life and is, at the same time, the history of the young mother whose fears and travails remain a lesson for the girl. The last section of the poem, however, asserts the ultimate failure of speech between mothers and children.

> It is true that we lie down on cowflops
> praying they'll turn into pillows.
> It is true that our mothers explode
> out of the snowballs of dreams
> or speak to us down the chimney
> saying our names above the wind
>
> or scrape their legs like crickets
> in the dead grass behind the toolshed
> tapping a code we can't read.

Women try to pass on a key to their daughters that somehow gets lost in the language they use; their "code" cannot be deciphered and their voices are relegated to dreams and the wind. The larger "lesson" of the title becomes both the existence of crucial knowledge and its incommunicability.

Kumin again considers the way gender can defeat the connection between women in the poem that follows "History Lesson." In "The Thirties Revisited," Kumin uses a child's persona to examine the adolescent girl's rite of passage, menarche, and its effect on her isolation. The opening stanzas establish the girl's sympathy with dying animals— a bleeding horse, shot squirrels—in order to evoke her own sense of biological victimization and wounding. These vignettes are formally linked by a repeated refrain from a child's rhyming game, the old riddle whose answer is always set up to be "Pinch me." The refrain captures the sense of the child's world that the girl still partially inhabits, as well as her pain and confusion adjusting to a woman's sexual body. Complicating this is the mother's rejection of her daughter because she lacks the proper physical and social attributes of femininity. Overwhelmed, the girl expresses her failures as a woman and daughter in a devastating picture.

> If daughters were traded among the accessories
> in the perfumed hush of Bonwit Teller's
> she'd have replaced me with a pocketbook,
> snapped me shut and looped me over
> her Hudson seal cuff: me of the chrome-wire mouth,
> the inkpot braids, one eye that looks
> wrongly across at the other.

Further, at menarche, the mother withdraws entirely from her daughter. This not only leaves the girl unprepared to cope with its meaning, but it becomes connected with loss of female affection and awareness of death. The speaker understandably develops fear and guilt over this turning point in her sexual identity, coming to womanhood with a sense of self-disgust and estrangement. The inane refrain now becomes a nightmarish image of gender.

> This is the year that my mother stiffens.
> She undresses in the closet giving me
> her back as if I can't see
> her breasts fall down like pufferfish,
> the life gone out of their crusty eyes.
> But who has punctured the bathroom light?
> Why does the mattress moan at night
> and why is nothing good
> said of all this business to come
> —the elastic belt with its metal tongue—
> when my body, that surprise,
> claps me into my first blood?

> Adam and Eve and Pinch Me Dead
> coasted down Strawberry Hill on a sled.
> Adam and Eve fell off in the mud
> but who do you think got covered with blood?

Kumin elevates another bit of family history to emblematic status in "Life's Work," when she compares herself and her mother at eighteen, a point of transition in identity and career. Her theme is the clash of women's self-determination with acceptable social roles; she finds defeat in her mother's abandoned desire to be a concert pianist, a career overruled by her autocratic father, and she sees a muted victory in her own life as a poet.

> my daddy wearing gravy on his face
> swore on the carrots and boiled beef
> that I would come to nothing
> that I would come to grief . . .

> Well, the firm, old fathers are dead
> and I didn't come to grief.
> I came to words instead
> to tell the little tale that's left:
> the midnights of my childhood still go on
> the stairs speak again under your foot
> the heavy parlor door folds shut
> and "Au Clair de la Lune"
> puckers from the obedient keys
> plain as a schoolroom clock ticking
> and what I hear more clearly than Debussy's
> lovesong is the dry aftersound
> of your long nails clicking.

It is a marvelously resonant passage. As the colon establishes, the tale that's left for the daughter to tell is the symbolic fate of the mother, whose dream of becoming a concert pianist has been reduced to solitary concerts late at night in the parlor. The clock image signifies the passage of years; the irony of the love song she chooses is that she had no choice at all, as the poem demonstrates, in the marriage that ended her musical ambitions. Her long nails, a disaster for serious piano playing, indicate a conventional feminine vanity superseding the importance of the music. The "clicking" sound that lingers in the daughter's mind echoes the dry crickets tapping at the end of "History Lesson." The entire scene evokes the waste of passion and ability in this woman's life brought on by "the firm, old fathers" against whom the daughter struggles, but with more success. Again, this is a significant advance over an early victimization poem like "Voice from the Roses," in which Kumin was unable to understand her mother in a context of roles and restrictions. In these poems of *House, Gate, Fountain, Bridge*, she makes that extension.

IV

The trend to personalization continues strongly in *The Retrieval System*, which is dedicated to her daughters. Perhaps she feels she can pass on in her poetry what is so often incommunicable in person. Her conviction that the mother-daughter relationship is fated to be misunderstood and mutually alienating does not alter. In "Parting," she unsparingly describes parents seeing their daughter off at the airport: the couple stand "like toys / wound up once or twice" and then shunted aside. Their forlorn "commonplace constellation" is, to the poet, "the celestial arrangement." Kumin's own daughters are gone from her in various postures of relief or estrangement. Her love for them seems inarticulate, "too tense or too lax" as Bogan put it, her gestures ambivalent and her love private. Thinking of one of her daughters, she admits,

> She is all uncertainties,
> as I am in this mothering business.
>
> . . . .
>
> We bulge toward separate fates that await us
> Sometimes touching, as sleeves will, whether
> or not a hug was intended.
> ("Sunbathing on a Rooftop in Berkeley")

She writes as a parent of children in general, "Soon enough, no matter how / we want them to be happy / . . . Fury slams in / The willful fury befalls." Out of the legacy of baffled love and anger emerge people who cannot bridge their separateness and who fall into civil rhythms of inconsequential remarks and restraint.

> Eventually we get them back.
> Now they are grown up.
> They are much like ourselves.
> They wake mornings beyond cure,
> not a virgin among them.
> We stand in the kitchen
> slicing bread, drying spoons,
> and tuning in to the weather.
> ("Changing the Children")

In "The Envelope," Kumin uses the image of Russian dolls of descending size who fit inside each other to parallel the continuation of mothers inside their daughters' lives. Riding into eternity like "an arrested fetus" or "a chain letter good for the next thousand years," mothers are helplessly, lovingly, yet awfully, internalized by their daughters.

For relief from the emotional tangle of intimacy, Kumin turns again to the figure of the solitary, who has compelled her throughout her work. Exemplified by the hermit in *Up Country*, he now emerges in *The Retrieval System* as Henry Manley, a character who made one earlier appearance in *The Nightmare Factory*. Whereas the Hermit is mythic in his balance and integration, Henry is a more realistic persona, a tough New England farmer living up the road from the poet in Warner, New Hampshire. There is an enviable grit in his self-sufficiency, but Kumin does not evade his capitulation to age and loneliness. While praising "Henry's rich example" in the reclusive life he leads, she also sees "his view of things fall in." Still, her own withdrawn existence in the rural eastern landscape remains a crucial part of her voice and themes. The final section of *The Retrieval System* is devoted to poems about her routine in this locale. Generally, they exude a stronger personal peace than those that refer to social and personal ties.

Despite the title, this collection dwells on irretrievability. In the title poem, the opening recollections are fond and perceptive as the speaker notes the unaccountable fact that animals and strangers assume the faces and quirks of dead loved ones. Yet, as the poem continues and the memories of deaths mount, its mood becomes increasingly bleak and morbid. She has to stop herself with, "I don't want to brood." But the brooding is there, and by the end the tone is elegiac and ominous. "The forecast is nothing but trouble. / It will snow fiercely enough to fill all these open graves." The possible allusion to James Joyce's "The Dead" intensifies the poem's disturbing sense of cold and catastrophe. The graves are "open," people do not stay dead; instead they return strangely, unsettlingly. This is the subject of earlier Kumin poems, especially those to her dead father in *The Privilege*. The protean quality of the dead frustrates the ability of the living to reach a quittance with grief. The frustration is yet another dimension of isolation.

Kumin's poems to Anne Sexton continue to pursue the subject of death and guilt. The suicide of her closest friend leaves her with emotions she cannot resolve. In "July, Against Hunger," she thinks of how "loneliness fills me like a pitcher. / The old deaths dribble out." The poem concludes with an apprehension of "the Rat," death, "who comes all winter to gnaw on iron / or wood, and tears the last flesh from the bone." The dominant tone of this collection is summed up by the moody, stark lines in "Address to the Angels"—"Always / I think that no one / can be sadder than I am." Isolation remains the overwhelming center of existence. "We are, each one of us, our own / prisoner. We are / locked up in our own story."

The early work of Kumin continues the themes and formal stylistic concerns of Bogan—the threatening forces of disintegration and loss, the fragility of happiness, the constant awareness of death. Yet, to Bogan's comprehensive sense of betrayal, Kumin brings in her later poetry a trust in the land and its creatures, and a greater awareness of the sharing of pain. Kumin's sense of her context in family patterns, of her development in relation to specific people, events, and locales, increases through her writing and saves her from Bogan's victimizing feeling of singularity. Also, unlike Bogan, Kumin does not seek to control nature, or make it an emotional colony of the mind. Her respect for the precise details of the external landscape is a measure of her need to hold on to reality, much as Marlow scrupulously attends to his broken engine in Joseph Conrad's *Heart of Darkness*. Visually holding on to things functions as a barrier against what she calls "this history of loss."

In her middle work, she moves away from formal structures toward a poetic style that depends on deft description, a strong narrative line, and the present tense. Even many of Kumin's poems about her childhood are written as if their events were presently occurring. Her comfort with the present tense stems from her desire to hold on to the real and the immediate. Movements into past and future tenses in her poems almost always signal a confrontation with death. She habitually controls these movements through the use of subjunctive or imperative moods, to create a vision that neutralizes or rejects the real but negative future. These wish poems in her work express a celebration and joy that is usually missing in the present. Her series of Hermit poems do capture a feeling of existing joy combined with, and even founded on, a positive isolation that approaches validation. Yet these, too, are more properly classified as wish poems, since they are only possible through the projection of a male persona in a mythic landscape. Nevertheless, in her own life, Kumin has moved closer and closer to the physical realities of the mythical Hermit. She confessed to an interviewer that if it were not for the necessity to lecture and tour to make money to satisfy the needs of herself and her beloved horses, she could forego human society almost totally.[17] If she had it to do over again, she now doubts whether she would ever marry, even though her own marriage has happily survived. Her life, bounded by the demands and rewards of her farm, fulfills her and she resents having to spend time away from the farm. She admits, "I have this big thing about wanting to be totally self-sufficient," perhaps urged on by the memory of those years when the needs and feelings of others always came first.[18] "Now I would say for the first time in my life I'm doing what I've always wanted to do, almost without strictures. It's awfully nice to have grown-up children who are out there on their own and are not relying on you heavily emotionally . . . and you can begin to exploit life in a way. I suddenly feel as if I've come into a really selfish time. And I love it. I guard it jealously; I don't want to give up any of it."[19]

Kumin's isolation remains finally both fated and willed, and through her poetic recapitulation of the past and her personal place in it, her isolation is also understood and accepted. It is a compelling mixture of

17. Litwack, "A Conversation," 70.
18. Meek, "An Interview," 318.
19. Litwack, "A Conversation," 66.

faith and grief; she is, as she says, "a rescuer by temperament," but the crop she tenderly covers, like the life she carefully hoards, is only imperfectly kept from loss. "Outdoors the tomato plants under their old bedsheets have taken on the outlines of white dinosaurs. It is all in vain. Nothing green can be had in trade this night. The horses sleep standing up, silently growing their winter coats as a hard frost rides in leaving a trail of white prints on the grass, the rooftop, the forgotten handbook of mushrooms left open to dog stinkhorn."[20]

20. Maxine Kumin, "Wintering Over," in Kumin, *To Make a Prairie: Essays on Poets, Poetry, and Country Living* (Ann Arbor, 1979), 169.

III / Homespun and Crazy Feathers

THE SPLIT-SELF IN THE POEMS OF DENISE LEVERTOV

When I am the sky
a glittering bird
slashes at me with knives of song.

When I am the sea
fiery clouds plunge into my mirrors,
fracture my smooth breath with crimson sobbing.

When I am the earth
I feel my flesh of rock wearing down:
pebbles, grit, finest dust, nothing.

When I am a woman—O, when I am
a woman,
my wells of salt brim and brim,
poems force the lock of my throat.
DENISE LEVERTOV
"Cancion"

The term *split-self* was first given significance for women's poetry in
Florence Howe's introduction to *No More Masks*.[1] It describes an opposition women feel between essential aspects of the self, between
what is socially prescribed on the basis of gender and what is defined
on the basis of self, between what a woman feels she should be and
what she feels she is. Denise Levertov has written a substantial number
of poems exploring this duality, the pain and frustration of which
often belie the joyous poet, celebrating the world and self, she is generally taken to be. Levertov particularly identifies the two selves with the
domestic gender role and the artist. The former occupies a safe position, accepted and esteemed by society in general and males in particular, while her counterpart haunts the fringes of human intercourse,
isolated from men and women alike, and repressed by the woman of
whose psyche she is part.

The traditional female is associated with the enclosed world of the
household, kitchen, and bedroom. In her guise as mother, wife, and
helpmate, she exhibits a basic passivity and immobility that Levertov

1. Florence Howe, "Introduction," in Florence Howe and Ellen Bass (eds.), *No More
Masks: An Anthology of Poems by Women* (New York, 1973), 27–33.

characteristically reinforces with images of sleeping. The artist, however, inhabits an unbounded world of independence, movement, and vitality; her freedom and power can be both stimulating and threatening. Her symbols are the moon, the forest, water, and places of mystery, imagination, and ritual. Unlike the relatively static domestic self, the artist initiates actions, undertakes journeys. Choices made by this self in favor of uncertainty, even pain, become artistic choices and entail the necessity of confronting unfamiliar experiences and environments, unlike those of security and ease in which the domestic self rests. Yet, the artist appears in clothes and circumstances that stamp her as an indifferent mother, a poor housekeeper, a woman whose disregard of social conventions keeps her an exotic, eccentric figure. These dichotomies are not unique, certainly, to Levertov, either in their particular traits or in the split-self strategy, but she is worthy of focus for the persistence of the theme in her work and for the paradigm she presents for examining both the repression and resolution possible through such poems.

It is important to distinguish the images of enclosure and passivity connected to the gender role from images of victimization. Levertov as an artist may struggle against the enervating or limiting influence of the gender role, but as a mother, wife, and woman in her society, she is also powerfully drawn to it. Significantly, she rarely portrays this self as a victim. To society and to herself, the figure, compounded of what Woolf called "the angel in the house" and what Tillie Olsen calls "the essential, maintenance-of-life angel," has the full weight of tradition and cultural approbation behind her. The "angel" in Levertov's poetry is not weak, bitter, or isolated, nor does Levertov caricature her in any way that would trivialize the tremendous pressure she exerts against the competing artist self. It is the latter who carries the burden of guilt, fear, and alienation for her rebellion. Clearly this split carries implications for male and female relationships in the poems, since it is the power of the masculine, patriarchal world that stands most firmly behind the persuasive cultural power of the gender roles enacted by the self. Frequently, poems in which Levertov writes of her isolation from a particular lover are at heart manifestations of the split-self. In these poems the man, who is the spokesman for the domestic self, implicitly exerts pressure on the woman to be passive and dependent and to fulfill her role, while the artist self struggles for validation and freedom.

Anais Nin wrote in her journals what is perhaps one of the most moving statements of the dilemma of conflicting selves in the woman writer, wherein her desire to be loved by men, to be accepted by culture as womanly, rises up to silence the power and voice of the artist.

I did not want to rival man. . . . I must protect them [sic], not outshine them. . . . I did not want to steal man's creation, his thunder.

Creation and femininity seemed incompatible. The *aggressive* act of creation.

. . . To create seemed to me such an assertion of the strongest part of me that I would no longer be able to give all those I love the feeling of their being stronger, and they would love me less.

An act of independence would be punished by desertion. I would be abandoned by all those I loved.

Men fear women's strength. I have been deeply aware of men's weakness, the need to guard them from my strength.

I have made myself less powerful, have concealed my powers.

. . . I have concealed my abilities like an evil force that would overwhelm, hurt, or weaken others.

I have crippled myself.

Dreams of Chinese women with bound feet.

I have bound myself spiritually.

I have associated creation with ruthlessness, absence of scruples, indifference to consequences.

. . . The creator's guilt in me has to do with my femininity, my subjection to man.

Also with my maternal self in conflict with my creative self.

. . . Guilt about exposing the father.

Secrets.

Need of disguises.

Fear of consequences.

Great conflict here.[2]

The long, slow cadence of the beginning builds to a litany of confession, a lamentation of loss and mutilation of the self in its fundamental

2. Anais Nin, entry for January, 1943, in *The Diaries of Anais Nin: Volume III*, cited in Jeanette Webber and Joan Grumman (eds.), *Woman as Writer* (Boston, 1978), 36–37.

aspects, maternal and artistic, dutiful and powerful, communal and solitary. The terse, almost telegraphic language at the end comes like cries of grief. These griefs, the "great conflict" of which Nin so eloquently writes, flow through Levertov's poetry.

Denise Levertov was born October 24, 1923, in London, and spent her girlhood in suburban Ilford, Essex. It was a stimulating, intellectual household, her father being a respected Hasidic scholar and her mother strongly Welsh in background. Levertov and her elder sister, Olga, never attended public schools but were educated privately at home by their parents and tutors. For a time Levertov pursued serious work as a ballerina, and later she served as a nurse during World War II. Her first collection of poetry, *The Double Image*, was published in 1946 by the Cresset Press in London. In 1947, she married Mitchell Goodman, an American novelist. They lived in France, Mexico, and Maine, and eventually settled in New York City with their son, Nikolai, where they lived until their divorce in 1974.

From the beginning, Levertov's poetry demonstrates a continuity of theme and expression concerning central divisions in the self. Her work is a compelling account of the presence of the split, but also of manifold efforts to disguise it, minimize it, dissociate herself from its power. Even *The Double Image*, which most critics tend to pass over as too youthful and derivative to consider with Levertov's "real" work, has hints of this theme. Levertov, who confesses to having been embarrassed later by *The Double Image*, has developed a new appreciation of the ties between her first book and her maturer work, stating simply, "I have always—even in the muzzy adolescent vagueness of *The Double Image*—written out of my own experience as I grasped it, so that the field has grown larger as I walked through it, one might say, but yes, it is the same field."[3] The very title of the book points to an awareness of duplicity in vision, a duality in life and perception. The morbidity of the book issues partly from its backdrop of war, partly from its derivative romanticism, but there is a significant continuity in the poet's pessimistic rendering of lovers doomed to mutual isolation through the masks they assume or the blindness they exhibit in attempting to un-

3. Ian Reid, "Everyman's Land: An Interview with Denise Levertov," *Southern Review*, n.s., VIII (1972), 236.

derstand each other. This situation appears in such poems as "For B. M.," "Return," "Meditation and Voices," "Barricades," "The Dreamers," and "Two Voices." In "Two Voices," the result is a type of split-self poem. It could be read as a conventional dialogue poem between personifications of life and death or dynamic and static aspects of nature, or more interestingly, as a poem in which the woman speaker is trying to tell her lover what her inner self is truly like. Against his protestations, which emphasize her as the quiet, beautiful feminine ideal he beholds, she asserts the harsher reality of her turbulent artist self. The two voices represent the divergent views of her womanness.

> What can I give you? I am the unseizable
> indigo and wandering sea. I give
> no love but music, cold and terrible airs
> to darken on your heart as albatross
> obscures the gleaming water with a wing.
>
> *Be silent. You are beautiful; I hear*
> *only the summer whisper on the shore.*
>
> What can I give you? I am that great tree,
> the green penumbra of forgotten dreams.
> I send a leaf to greet you, but no more;
> my branches rustle in the wind of death.
>
> *Be still; I hear no menace in the wind;*
> *the tree is mine, and grows about my heart.*
>
> I am the wind. *I hold you.* I am gone,
> shade of no substance. What is it you hold?
> *Shadow, I love you.*
> Free me. I am death.

Levertov's conception here of the artist self contains the imagery she will return to again and again—coldness, darkness, wings, violent movement, a strong connection with natural elements, a sense of freedom and escape. Yet, at the same time, the artist's power is unwomanly ("cold and terrible airs"), threatening both to men (an "albatross"; "I give no love") and even, it is implied, to herself ("I am death"). What the man reinforces and persists in seeing is the opposite of the artist—

a static figure who is beautiful, "only the summer whisper on the shore," and without menace of any kind. To the man, this woman "is mine"; the woman responds, "Free me." Although the speaker claims great power and independence, she can only feel these compulsively, but not yet with joy. Because her qualities seem irreconcilable with the male's feminine ideal, she faces the isolation and torment of her gifts. Thus the stage is set for subsequent split-self poems wherein the choice is forged between being the artist or the loved one of others, between risky freedom and safe enclosure, wherein to be true to the self is to be dangerous to others.

Particularly through her early work—*The Double Image, Here and Now, Overland to the Islands*, and *With Eyes at the Back of Our Heads*—her fear and ambivalence toward the split predominate, coupled with attempts to deny it. In the middle period—from *The Jacob's Ladder* through *To Stay Alive*—Levertov begins to work toward achieving wholeness of purpose and identity in the split-self poems. At each stage appear poems of at least temporary resolution, where the split either balances tenuously or one self achieves ascendancy. It is this final sense of resolution that emerges in her more recent work, *The Freeing of the Dust* and *Life in the Forest*.[4] Having fully chosen the artist and worked through the guilt and anger of casting off the less authentic self, Levertov effectively moves beyond the need and urgency of split-self poems.

II

"The Dogwood" from *Overland to the Islands* is an excellent example of the early split-self poems wherein the speaker resists admitting the inner divisions and their implications.

> The sink is full of dishes. Oh well.
> Ten o'clock, there's no
> hot water.

4. Denise Levertov, *Here and Now* (San Francisco, 1956); *Overland to the Islands* (Highlands, N.C., 1958); *With Eyes at the Back of Our Heads* (Norfolk, Conn., 1960); *The Jacob's Ladder* (New York, 1961); *O Taste and See* (New York, 1964); *The Sorrow Dance* (New York,

The kitchen floor is unswept, the broom
has been shedding straws. Oh well.

The cat is sleeping, Nikolai is sleeping,
Mitch is sleeping, early to bed,
aspirin for a cold. Oh well.

No school tomorrow, someone for lunch,
4 dollars left from the 10—how did that go?
Mostly on food. Oh well.

I could decide
to hear some chamber music
and today I saw—what?
Well, some huge soft deep
blackly gazing purple
and red (and pale)
anemones. Does that
take my mind off the dishes?
And dogwood besides.
Oh well. Early to bed, and I'll get up
early and put
a shine on everything and write
a letter to Duncan later that will shine too
with moonshine. Can I make it? Oh well.

The opening stanzas succinctly capture the woman's domestic ennui and distraction. The only one awake in a house of sleepers, she is worrying about running the household, meeting social commitments, and having her son home from school. To each of these demands on her time, energy, and management her response is the same "Oh well." In the pivotal fourth stanza, her focus shifts for the first time from flat, laconic statements to sensuous poetic language. The dogwood of the title aligns with the anemones outside the house in a visual, suggestive environment that handicaps her attention to the more prosaic inside

1967); *Relearning the Alphabet* (New York, 1970); *To Stay Alive* (New York, 1971); *Footprints* (New York, 1972); *The Freeing of the Dust* (New York, 1974); *Life in the Forest* (New York, 1978).

environment represented by the house and family. Incipient tensions between them precipitate the need for a decision either to continue her poetic musings about the beauty that she willingly allows to distract her or to turn back to her duties inside—a decision in favor of her art or the demands of her domestic role. Her solution is unsatisfactory. She gets short-term relief by making no choice at all; she merely decides to go to bed early, temporarily silencing both selves.

The speaker has evaded confronting the oppositions in her life, evaded the nature of her boredom and inactivity, and unconvincingly postponed matters until the next day, when she will try to placate the voices by shining up both the furniture and her art. The final irony— besides the ludicrous comparison of a superficial gloss of furniture polish with the work of the imagination—lies in the fact that when at last she allows herself to indulge her poetic images and thoughts, it is in a letter to a male poet (the reference is to Robert Duncan). She will make an effort to impress him with her "shine" (as she tries to satisfy her husband by being a good housekeeper), instead of directing her energy and insights into creating her own poem. Her world in miniature in this poem is a constant, depleting effort to shine for a male domestic and literary world and to deflect her instincts to write a poetry of her own. The consequences of this deflection, as the poem demonstrates, are inner contradictions, distractions (note the chopped phrasings, the interruptions and questions), weariness, and, worst of all, silence. Hence her final question, "Can I make it?," resonates with the desperation of all she is struggling to do: to satisfy her social roles, to keep alive her imagination, to maintain contact with the artistic world, and lastly to survive at all, to "make it," with so many claims upon her. Her response is one final "Oh well," at once bitter, nonchalant, and still maddeningly evasive. This phrase, repeated some seven times in the relatively short poem, acquires a complexity by the end, forcing one's attention to the pun. Often in her work Levertov uses the image of the well, frequently with female connotations, to refer to sources of poetic inspiration. Thus, the colloquial phrase functions as an embedded apostrophe to her buried self and her poetic power, both in danger of disappearing under the multiple pressures of gender roles. "The Dogwood" is a deceptively simple imagistic and syntactic elucidation of Tillie Olsen's conviction that women, through traditional socialization, have been made "mediocre caretakers of their own talent: that is, writing not first. . . . It is distraction, not meditation, that becomes habitual; interruption, not continuity; spasmodic, not constant, toil. Work interrupted, deferred, postponed, makes blockage—at best lesser accomplishment. Unused capacities atrophy, cease to be."[5]

Another submerged split is apparent in the poem "The Absence," also in *Overland*. Here again the speaker, awake while her male partner sleeps, feels spiritually isolated, longing for something she cannot quite name.

> Here I lie asleep
> or maybe I'm awake yet—
>
> not alone—and yet
> it seems by moonlight
>
> I'm alone, hardly hearing
> a breath beside me. And those shadows
>
> on the wall indeed are
> not shadows but the
>
> featherweight dancing echoes
> of headlights sliding by.
>
> Here I lie and wonder
> what it is has left me, what element.
> I can't remember my dreams
> by morning.
>   Maybe, as Frazer tells,
>
> my soul flew out in that moment
> of almost sleep. If it should go
> back to the scenes and times
> of its wars and losses
>
> how would I ever lure it
> back? It would

---

5. Tillie Olsen, "One Out of Twelve: Women Who Are Writers in This Century," in Sara Ruddick and Pamela Daniels (eds.), *Working It Out* (New York, 1976), 331, 334. See also, for a further testament to the conflicts of writer and housekeeper, such comments as Katherine Mansfield's in a letter to John Middleton Murry. In Susan Koppelman Cornillon (ed.), *Images of Women in Fiction* (Bowling Green, Ohio, 1973), 108.

be looking for something, it would be
too concentrated to hear me.

O moon, watching everything,
delay it in the garden among the white flowers

until the cold air before sunrise
makes it glad to come back to me through the screens.

The speaker has a haunting sense of being literally and psychologically divided, missing some vital part of herself. She associates this absent element with her dreams and imagination, wondering if it may be her very soul that has left her for the more complex emotional landscape of the past. She seems to envy her soul its freedom and intensity (recall the distraction that plagued the speaker in "The Dogwood"), and fears her soul will not willingly return to the life she offers it. Although warm and safe, this world is also screened off and enclosed. The speaker hopes a delay among the garden and its white flowers will compel the soul's return, but this seems uncertain. Although dark and cold, the garden is also the only visually appealing place in the poem. As in "The Dogwood," the speaker outwardly dwells in ease and security (the peacefully sleeping households, the warm rooms, the shiny furniture), while an inner self exists in a landscape of mystery and threat (the anemones are dark, "blackly gazing," the dogwood has sacrificial connotations, the soul is out in the night chill). Levertov leaves little doubt, however, that the latter is the place where poems are found.

In her early collections, though, she remains unwilling to fully embrace the contradictions and difficulties of the divided self in her own person, preferring to submerge expressions of it or else to project it onto third persons, as in "The Earthwoman and the Waterwoman" (in *Here and Now*) and "Sunday Afternoon" (in *Overland*).

The Earthwoman and the Waterwoman

The earthwoman by her oven
　　tends her cakes of good grain.
The waterwoman's children
are spindle thin.

> The earthwoman
> has oaktree arms. Her children
> full of blood and milk
>   stamp through the woods shouting.
> The waterwoman
>   sings gay songs in a sad voice
>   with her moonshine children.
> When the earthwoman
> has had her fill of the good day
>   she curls to sleep in her warm hut
>   a dark fruitcake sleep
> but the waterwoman
>   goes dancing in the misty lit-up town
>   in dragon-fly dresses and blue shoes.

The split assumes definite shape and embodiment in these two—the angel-in-the-house, or earthwoman, and the exotic outsider, or waterwoman. The former is the admirable domestic, a good mother and cook, whose days are bounded by a "warm hut" and whose nights are given over to sleep. Her rootedness is symbolized by her "oaktree arms." Her opposite, the waterwoman, does not sleep, and dances through the town wearing dubious clothing. Her images are those of the (female) imagination—the moon and water. She is the singer, the poet, but she is also the outcast, since her behavior does not conform to the ideal of the domestic earthwoman. Levertov's attitude toward her is both envious and rejecting; the poet possesses freedom and vitality, but her children suffer and her voice is sad. The waterwoman's children are a likely reference to Levertov's poems, and the adjectives of insubstantiality ("thin," "moonshine") that describe them indicate her troubled sense of them. The paradox of "gay songs in a sad voice" is a reference to her inability to correlate experience with expression, the crisis of language caused by the split-self. In any case, Levertov still distances herself from the split by projecting it onto these folk forms and by using two women rather than a single woman divided against herself.

Another split-self poem, "Sunday Afternoon," draws on the contradictory socialization of young girls who are balanced at the point in

adolescence when they straddle the freedom and movement of childhood and the curtailment and passivity of womanhood.

> After the First Communion
> and the banquet of mangoes and
> bridal cake, the young daughters
> of the coffee merchant lay down
> for a long siesta, and their white dresses
> lay beside them in quietness
> and white veils floated
> in their dreams as the flies buzzed.
> But as the afternoon
> burned to a close they rose
> and ran about the neighborhood
> among the half-built villas
> alive, alive, kicking a basketball, wearing
> other new dresses, of blood-red velvet.

The first part mingles marriage symbols with overtones of death,
negatively prefiguring the passive feminine postures the girls inevitably must adopt, while the second half of the poem literally resurrects
them ("they rose / . . . alive, alive") back into a world of colors, passion, and freedom that is associated with masculine activity (the basket-
ball). The villas, "half-built," signal the enclosures already being erected
to contain these girls who "rose," "ran," and kicked but whose future is
to "lay," float, and dream.

Similar distinctions frame the poem "Something to Wear," from
Here and Now, but carry more pointed implications for the woman
poet.

> To sit and sit like the cat
> and think my thoughts through—
> that might be a deep pleasure:
>
> to learn what news
> persistence might discover,
> and like a woman knitting
> make something from the

skein unwinding, unwinding,
something I could wear

or something you could wear
when at length I rose to meet you
outside the quiet sitting-room

(the room of thinking and knitting
the room of cats and women)
among the clamor of

cars and people,
the stars drumming and poems
leaping from shattered windows.

The speaker defines two distinct feminine and masculine spheres. The former is quiet, still and passive, while the latter is full of activity, spectacle, exchange, and, significantly enough, poetry. She must rise from the feminine space (note the same verb used here as in "Sunday Afternoon" for passage between these worlds) to meet the man and write her poems. Even the thinking and persistence she envisions is only something that "might" occur in her room; it is a pleasure she has yet to "learn." But the world of poetry "shatters" the calm retreat of the speaker. It is not peaceful and repetitious like knitting, but various, clamorous, even violent—"stars drumming and poems / leaping from shattered windows."

A repeated problem in these poems and others through the early collections (for instance, "The Gypsy's Window," "Mrs. Cobweb," "Sharks") is that Levertov consistently locates poetry in realms that seem unavailable to her as a woman, realms she can only enter in disguise or by risking her status as a good, acceptable woman. The titles of both *Here and Now* and *Overland to the Islands* establish goals and means of poetic expression—full participation in the immediate world and in the quest—but the poems themselves tend to fall away from these ideals; Levertov cannot fully risk herself as a poet, since to do so is to risk also her society's concept of her as a woman. Thus, in *Here and Now*, the emphasis on an ethic of joyous immediacy falters in the split-self poems ("The Earthwoman and the Waterwoman," "Mrs. Cobweb," "The Gypsy's Window"), in poems in which the speaker cannot write what she wants ("The Rights") or in which she must repress her femininity to write ("Something to Wear"). Even in such love poems as "The Lovers," "Marriage," and "Marriage (II)," the woman does not experience the world firsthand in a participatory "here and now," but emerges mainly as a passive receiver of colors, images, and emotions brought to life for her by the intercession of a dominant male figure.

Similarly, in *Overland to the Islands*, the title poem sets out the motif of the eclectic journey as the proper undertaking of the artist. Yet, since the journey necessitates the very qualities that are attributes of the unacceptable self—movement, independence, and personal power —the poems tend to show the frustration and stagnation of the journey. It is no surprise, then, when Levertov writes of losing her direction, of being unable to communicate, in "The Dogwood" and "The Absence"; of activity that is merely frantic and purposeless, in "Merritt Parkway"; of being frightened off when she ventures into new regions, in "The Sharks"; and of crying out to the red flowers to rouse her anger and spirit when she is closed off by oppressive comfort and security, in "A Song." She remains essentially passive, hoping for some stronger force to rescue her. Because of pressure exerted by others and her own internalization of their values, she is unable to rebel successfully against the domestic self, and her poetry becomes an increasingly contradictory, problematic pursuit.

The result is a crisis of language: a poet who is dishonest to herself cannot be true to her art. "The Whirlwind," one of the final poems in *Overland*, explodes with the power of the struggle in the poet and forces the issue of the integrity of an art based on denial of half the artist's energy and instinct.

> The doors keep rattling—I
> stick poems between their teeth to
> stop them. The brown dust
> twirls up outside the window, off
> the dead jicama field, scares the curtains,
> spirals away to the dirty hollow
> where the cesspools are, and the most ants,
> and beyond—to the unfenced pasture land, where nothing
> will get in its way for miles and it
> can curtsey itself at last into

some arroyo. The doors
keep rattling—I'm
shivering, desperate for a poem
to stuff into their maws that will
silence them. I know what they want:
they want
in all their wooden strength
to fly off on the whirlwind into
the great nothingness.

The doors represent her threshold into the outer world, in the true
direction of her art and desires. The doors must fling open, just as the
windows of "Something to Wear" must shatter and the screens in "The
Absence" must be transited, in order that the enclosures and barriers
to her authentic self may be removed. The doors are like giant mouths
("maws," "teeth") symbolizing repressed expression that threatens to
burst forth. She wants to silence them with false poems but becomes
desperate when she cannot write them quickly enough. The irony is
that she is trying to use poems to disguise her experience (she knows
what the doors want), which itself prevents the poems from coming.
Poems open doors; they do not close them. The wind appears as a female power, possibly the muse, by the curious personification in line
10. The speaker is fighting her own power, turning one self (the silencing poems, the intact, safe enclosure) against the other self of open
doors, mystery, and presumably a more complex reality and experience. However, an allegiance between the two becomes more terrifying
the more she denies it, as show in the image of the whirlwind and the
projection onto it of her worst fears: isolation and nothingness.

The resolution of these early split-self poems is reached in the
strong poem, "The Goddess," from *With Eyes at the Back of Our Heads*
(published two years after *Overland to the Islands*), capping for the moment the intertwining crisis of language and self. Unable to take herself firmly enough in hand as a poet, unwilling to open the doors, so to
speak, the artist self is literally and decisively thrown out of her safe,
enclosed world by no less a figure than the Muse herself.

She in whose lipservice
I passed my time,

whose name I knew, but not her face,
came upon me where I lay in Lie Castle!

Flung me across the room, and
room after room (hitting the walls, re-
bounding—to the last
sticky wall—wrenching away from it
pulled hair out!)
till I lay outside the outer walls!

There in the cold air
lying still where her hand had thrown me,
I tasted the mud that splattered my lips:
asleep and growing! I tasted
her power!

The silence was answering silence,
a forest was pushing itself
out of sleep between my submerged fingers.

I bit on a seed and it spoke on my tongue
of day that shone already among stars
in the water-mirror of low ground,
and a wind rising ruffled the lights:
she passed near me returning from the encounter,
she who plucked me from the close rooms,

without whom nothing
flowers, fruits, sleeps in season,
without whom nothing
speaks in its own tongue, but returns
lie for lie!

This is an extraordinary denouement for a poet depleted by enclosures, domesticity, and dormant energies yet fearfully clinging to the
security these offered. She has implicitly cried out for a revolutioniz-
ing force but has been afraid to act. The Muse must literally haul and
maul her weak sister outside the walls of "Lie Castle," a poetry that has
become false to her needs and experience. The poet, from her new
position of freedom, can now admit the dishonesty and encoding of

her art: "She in whose lipservice / I passed my time, / whose name I knew but not her face . . . without whom nothing / speaks in its own tongue, but returns / lie for lie!" Everything that has become associated with the domestic self—sleep, warmth, walls, tidiness, passivity— violently reverses as the speaker lies splattered with mud out in the cold. A forest rousing from hibernation between her fingers suggests the new growth and force of her writing to come, while power stirs in her mouth under the stern injunction to tell the truth of her experience. Recalling the dramatic circumstances surrounding the poem's creation, Levertov writes, "'The Goddess' . . . is not based on a dream but on an actual waking vision. . . . The poem's energy arises from an experience of awakening to the truth and to the necessity for truthfulness—an experience sufficiently profound to produce the image of Truth as a Goddess and to produce that image spontaneously."[6]

III

"The Goddess" climaxes the sequence of split-self poems in Levertov's early work. In her next book, *The Jacob's Ladder* (1961), no split-self poems appear; however, her sixth book, *O Taste and See* (1964), picks up the theme again—in "In Mind" and "Melody Grundy," which recall figures like Mrs. Cobweb and the Waterwoman; in "Gone Away," a companion poem to "The Absence"; and in "Song for Ishtar," which, like "The Goddess," is another climactic resolution poem. Another poem in this volume, often anthologized, assumes the dynamics of the split-self without actually delineating the respective personae. "Hypocrite Women" acknowledges the disguises women adopt, the suppression they practice to preserve a patriarchal view of them that does not accurately reflect their lives and thoughts. Levertov has plainly acknowledged that while the poem "was written before the women's movement existed in present form, it's written in some recognition of how those stereotypes do in fact oppress one as a woman."[7] "Hypocrite

6. Denise Levertov, "The Sense of Pilgrimage," *The Poet in the World* (New York, 1973), 72–73.
7. Levertov was responding to an interviewer's remark that "Hypocrite Women" would not satisfy militant feminists. For her full answer, see Anthony Piccione and William Heyen, "A Conversation with Denise Levertov," *Ironwood*, IV (1973), 23.

Women" takes a harsher view of the gender role than most split-self poems, in which, however discomfiting this self might be, it is almost always treated with respect and sympathy. Instead, in "Hypocrite Women," Levertov comes down hard on the lies and misery perpetuated by women's continuing silence and self-trivialization. Again the split-self is connected to the crisis of women's language. Levertov emphasizes verbs of expression: "how seldom we speak"; "we are too much women to own to such unwomanliness"; "we say nothing of this later." Women are isolated from themselves, from each other, from men, and from language.

On the strength of this admission about women, which is also an admission about herself, Levertov follows "Hypocrite Women" with the poem "In Mind." This poem marks the first time she acknowledges the presence of the split in herself without efforts to submerge or deny it.

> There's in my mind a woman
> of innocence, unadorned but
>
> fair-featured, and smelling of
> apples or grass. She wears
>
> a utopian smock or shift, her hair
> is light-brown and smooth, and she
>
> is kind and very clean without
> ostentation—
>   but she has
> no imagination.
>   And there's a
> turbulent moon-ridden girl
>
> or old woman, or both,
> dressed in opals and rags, feathers
>
> and torn taffeta,
> who knows strange songs—
>
> but she is not kind.

In essence, the Earthwoman and Waterwoman have reappeared, with the important difference being the poet's personal avowal of the split.

Still present is the ambivalence toward the artist, whose decisiveness, after "The Goddess," seems to have fallen into doubt again. The poet, retaining her stigmas of ostracism and bad temper, has improved little over her earlier delineations.

If "In Mind" seems a throwback to past struggles, at least "Song for Ishtar," the opening poem of the volume, throws its weight with full force on the side of the "moon-ridden girl."

> The moon is a sow
> and grunts in my throat
> Her great shining shines through me
> so the mud of my hollow gleams
> and breaks in silver bubbles.
>
> She is a sow
> and I a pig and a poet
>
> When she opens her white
> lips to devour me I bite back
> and laughter rocks the moon
>
> In the black of desire
> we rock and grunt, grunt and
> shine.

As in "The Goddess," the poet confronts her muse, though the poet has now increased in confidence and aggressiveness, as Levertov chooses the artist self without qualification, ambivalence, or guilt. The poem is a rich celebration of feminine power and creativity that embraces the crude and the spiritual, the physical and the psychic, both "pig" and "poet." Playing on the old folk belief of the moon's ability to impregnate women, the interaction of the poet with her muse uses language and motions of sexuality to achieve an epiphany of self-fertilization, whereby the poet creates out of her own self and power: "the mud of my hollow gleams / and breaks in silver bubbles." Levertov is not afraid to characterize the artist as exotic or coarse, or to overturn cultural signposts of feminine appeal by calling herself a pig. Indeed the overtones of the poem suggest a retreat not only from men's gender expectations but from men as sexual partners. The woman alone, or in

partnership with her muse, is explosively sexual. The poet has reached
a fullness of creative and natural independence in her raucous, shining identification with a female cosmos.

   Just as "Song for Ishtar" opens the collection *O Taste and See*, a split-
self poem, "The Wings," opens her next book, *The Sorrow Dance* (1967),
and plays again on familiar patterns: oppositions of vulnerability and
power, immobility and flight, female and male, death and birth. The
central tension revolves around the unknown contents of a heavy black
hump the speaker carries on her back.

> Something hangs in back of me,
> I can't see it, can't move it.
>
> I know it's black,
> a hump on my back.
>
> It's heavy. You
> can't see it.
>
> What's in it? Don't tell me
> you don't know. It's
>
> what you told me about—
> black
>
> inimical power, cold
> whirling out of it and
>
> around me and
> sweeping you flat.
>
> But what if,
> like a camel, it's
>
> pure energy I store,
> and carry humped and heavy?
>
> Not black, not
> that terror, stupidity
>
> of cold rage; or black
> only for being pent there?
>
> What if released in air
> it became a white

> source of light, a fountain
> of light? Could all that weight
>
> be the power of flight?
> Look inward: see me
>
> with embryo wings, one
> feathered in soot, the other
>
> blazing ciliations of ember, pale
> flare-pinions. Well—
>
> could I go
> on one wing,
>
> the white one?

The initial descriptions emphasize the weight and mystery of the woman's encumbrance; the hump suggests something of both a witch's physical deformity and her magic sack. Its repellent aspects are stressed by the "you," who is probably male, in terms characteristic of male denigration of witches and powerful women: "Black inimical power," unwomanly coldness, and unnatural strength (power capable of sweeping the man flat). He resorts to other common terms of dismissing a woman's force as "stupidity," "terror," or "cold rage." His impulse is to fear and negate the hidden part of the speaker. The woman, however, looks for the other, more positive possibilities in herself, though her style of bemused interrogation makes this dissension from the man's opinion almost apologetic. She asks five questions about the nature of this appendage; under her effort to redefine it, the hump assumes connotations of a birth sack, "humped and heavy" containing "embryo wings." The heavy, old self might shed to reveal new movement and beauty, "the power of flight." The climax of the poem is the speaker's imperative to the man, "Look inward: see me." It is an injunction both to look deeply into himself to see the misconceived image of her he harbors there, and into her to recognize her heretofore disguised but authentic self. Still, the poem concludes unsatisfactorily in a way reminiscent of "The Dogwood." The series of questions, the parenthetical "Well," and the irresolution in the final lines leave the speaker wondering if she can make it on one white wing alone, since she feels compelled to reject the black one (colored with cultural fears and apprehensions). The questions, as well as the continuing split, protect the speaker and the man from the full assertion of her power, but they limit it, too.

The centerpiece of *The Sorrow Dance* is the long sequence, broken into six sections, titled the "Olga Poems." These present the painful process of Levertov's coming to terms with the death of her older sister in 1964. The sequence recounts the troubled relationship between the two sisters, from their great intimacy in childhood to the years of eventual alienation and distance. Olga, the older by nine years, was from the beginning a figure of power and authority in her younger sister's eyes. She taught her music, fantasy, ideas, and stories; her presence dominated their childhood world. Throughout her later life, however, Olga was on uneven terms with her family and only sister, largely as a result of her political fervor and willful temperament. In the "Olga Poems," Levertov speaks of her sister's "rage" and "dread," which apparently collapsed gradually into an embattled, paranoid personality that finally estranged her from everyone.

The "Olga Poems" function as memoriam, but they are also, perhaps unconsciously to the poet, a continued working out of the split-self duality in the persons of the two very distinct sisters, Denise and Olga Levertov. In this projection, Olga becomes the isolated artist self, and Denise becomes the well-behaved, traditionally feminine girl. The image patterns throughout the poem support this interpretation. Olga is described with the same adjectives and details that have become linked with the artist in previous split-self poems. The opening stanzas begin to distinguish the two sisters along the lines of the familiar division.

> By the gas-fire, kneeling
> to undress,
> scorching luxuriously, raking
> her nails over olive sides, the red
> waistband ring—
>
> (And the little sister
> beady-eyed in the bed—
> or drowsy, was I? My head
> a camera—)
> Sixteen. Her breasts

> round, round, and
> dark-nippled—

Olga, the exotic, sensual sister, luxuriates in the warmth and in her body, while the other sister watches in circumspect fascination from the bed. Olga is described as having dark physical coloring, another distinction between the selves, since frequently in Levertov's poems the traditional woman is fair, while the artist is dark or associated with vibrant colors. Another early difference between the sisters was their social conscience; Olga's empathy for human suffering left Levertov unmoved.

> . . . human shame swept you
> when you were nine and saw
> the Ley Street houses,
>
> grasping their meaning as *slum*.
> Where I, reaching that age,
> teased you, admiring
>
> architectural probity, circa
> eighteen-fifty, and noted
> pride in the whitened doorsteps.

Olga's imaginative and artistic pursuits seem foremost in Levertov's recollection of their childhood relationship. She puts words to music, sight-reads the Beethoven sonatas, composes verses, sings songs with her sister, and fantasizes adventures for the two of them during long walks and long days in the park. The only difficulty with seeing Olga in these poems as the artist self is Levertov's own attitude toward her sister: she seems to reject and dissociate herself from the very characteristics which distinguish Olga as an artist. The suspicion arises that Levertov is most uncomfortable with the unwomanly, unfeminine aspects of her sister. For instance, she is put off by Olga's high-pitched voice, her "nagging insistence," her "picking those endless arguments," her intellectualism ("*Everything flows* / she muttered into my childhood"). Above all, she is uncomfortable with her sister's intensity and assertiveness.

> The high pitch of
> nagging insistence, lines
> creased into raised brows—

Ridden, ridden—
the skin around the nails
nibbled sore—

You wanted
to shout the world to its senses,
did you?—to browbeat

the poor into joy's
socialist republic—
What rage

Curiously, the details and terms she uses to convey her sister's personality are reminiscent of the negative sanctions used against the artist
self elsewhere in Levertov's poems and traditionally used against
women for being unfeminine and masculine.

Black one, incubus—
    she appeared
riding anguish as Tartars ride mares

over the stubble of the bad years.

In one of the years
    when I didn't know if she were dead or alive
I saw her in dream

haggard and rouged
    lit by the flare
from an eel—or cockle-stand on a slum street—

was it a dream? I had lost

all sense, almost, of
    who she was, what—inside her skin,
under the black hair
                        dyed blonde—
it might feel like to be, in the wax and wane of
    the moon

By the end of the "Olga Poems," Levertov has not really expressed
an understanding of, or admiration for, her sister. This occurs, how-

ever, with some conviction in two poems that appear later in *The Sorrow Dance* and in the facts of Levertov's life. One of the poems that serves as a sort of epilogue to the memoriam, "A Note to Olga (1966)," recounts Levertov's arrest during a demonstration against the Vietnam War. The conclusion approaches a point of emotional and psychological identity with her dead sister, as Levertov feels in herself the stirring power of an ardent political commitment. Almost unconsciously her life has begun to assume more affinity with Olga's.

> Though I forget you
> a red coal from your fire
> burns in that box.
>
> On the Times Square sidewalk
> we shuffle along, cardboard signs
> —Stop the War—
> slung around our necks.
>
> . . . .
> —It seems
> you that is lifted
>
> limp and ardent
> off the dark snow
> and shoved in, and driven away.

Levertov came to see the epilogic nature of this poem after *The Sorrow Dance*. When the "Olga Poems" were reprinted in *To Stay Alive* (1970), her overtly political, antiwar book, "A Note to Olga" was placed immediately following the sequence.

The second poem, though, is a far more intriguing afterword, at once more subtle and comprehensive than "Note to Olga." The poem, "A Vision," describes an almost archetypal dream of two powerful angels stopped in mid-flight at the sight of each other. "These two"

> so far as angels may dispute, were poised
> on the brink of dispute, brink of
> fall from angelic stature,
>
> . . . .
> These two hovered dazed before one another,
> for one saw the seafeathered, peacock breakered

> crests of the other angel's magnificence,
> different from his own,
>
> and the other's eyes flickered with vision of
> flame petalling, cream-gold grainfeather glitterings,
> the wings of his fellow

This poem is a symbolic enactment of the confrontation Levertov had desired with her sister, but missed. Levertov, whose element and colors are associated with water, is a blue-green angel, and Olga, whose element is fire and whose colors are red, brown, and gold, is a flame-colored angel. (Twice in the "Olga Poems," Levertov visualizes her sister by fires; she repeatedly associates her with the earth and its hues, and is fascinated by her eyes, which she describes as gold—"Your eyes were the brown gold of pebbles under water"; "gold brown eyes"; "gold gravel.") In "A Vision," at the mediating distance of the dream, the sisters come face-to-face with their mingled envy, anger, and love. Their hate can pull them down into eternal, mutually destructive divisiveness; their love can raise them to a new level of awareness of their beauty—a recognition between women, of women. At the climax of the dream, "the intelligence proper to great angels flew into their wings":

> So that each angel was iridescent with the strange newly-seen
> hues he watched; and their discovering pause
> and the speech their silent interchange of perfection was
>
> never became a shrinking to opposites,
>
> and they remained free in the heavenly chasm

IV

"Never became a shrinking to opposites"—this is precisely what the recurring split-self poems had threatened. Now, through the exhaustive emotional recapitulation of her sister's life and her own connections to that life, Levertov achieves an understanding and healing in "A Vision" that allows her finally to "remain free" of self-defeating reduction. Her new vision of wholeness, built on "newly seeing," preserves her from a fruitless polarization of emotions and capacities. "A

Vision" significantly marks the end of the split-self as it has been worked out in its various manifestations. This form appears only twice after *The Sorrow Dance*: in "Embroidery (I)," from *Relearning the Alphabet* (1970), and "The Woman," from *The Freeing of the Dust* (1975). Moreover, in an interesting development, each time it occurs the pairs are sisters.

"Embroidery (I)," built on the folktale of the two sisters, Rose White and Rose Red, uses imagery familiar from earlier split-self poems. Rose Red, the domestic self, prepares dinner, tends the hearth, and waits for the bear's return, while Rose White, the artist, sits to one side, her grey eyes looking off into the forest, away from the warm room. Rose Red, true to her name, has an "ardent, joyful / compassionate heart," attuned to the needs of the male bear, while her sister is "pale, turning away when she hears / the bear's paw on the latch." It is not the bear, but the "scent of the forest" in his fur, the air of the outside world, that fascinates Rose White. Later, in their beds, Rose Red falls into the customary sleep of the domestic self, dreaming "she is combing the fur of her cubs / with a golden comb." But in the posture characteristic of the artist, Rose White lies awake. In these particulars the poem is similar to other poems of its type, but it is more charming and fanciful. However, some remarkable distinctions become apparent on closer scrutiny. There is no perceivable tension between the Roses, nor does either hinder the other's pursuits. Rather than a split they appear as a unit, exemplified by the song they sing together.

> it is a cradle song, a loom song,
> a song about marriage, about
> a pilgrimage to the mountains
> long ago.

The song embraces "opposites"—motherhood (cradle) and artistry (loom), domesticity (marriage) and exploration (a pilgrimage to the mountains)—the directions hitherto presented as irreconcilable in Levertov's poetry. Moving further toward the new sense of resolution and inclusion, "Embroidery (I)" closes with the forecast of Rose White's marriage to the bear's brother "when the time is ripe." The selves coexist peacefully, singing together, and each shall marry in her own time; their unprecedented sisterhood betokens new strength and possibility.

Similarly in "The Women," though the selves are one person, they are implicitly sisters, characterized more by the solidarity between them than by their differences.

> It is the one in homespun
> you hunger for
> when you are lonesome;
>
> the one in crazy feathers
> dragging opal chains in dust
> wearies you
>
> wearies herself perhaps
> but has to drive on
> clattering rattletrap into
>
> fiery skies for trophies,
> into the blue that is bluer
> because of the lamps
>
> the silence keener because it is solitude
> moving through multitude on the night streets.
>
> But the one in homespun
> whom you want is weary
> too, wants to sit down
>
> beside you neither silent
> nor singing, in quietness. Alas,
> they are not two but one,
>
> pierce the flesh of one, the other
> halfway across the world, will shriek,
> her blood will run. Can you endure
> life with two brides, bridegroom?

The selves seem nearly identical in their characteristics to the women in "In Mind" except for the extraordinary empathy that now binds them. If one is pierced, the other will bleed; they are "two brides," suggesting new life and new emotional fidelities, and both are "weary" of the old, divisive relationship. The women are aligned with themselves; it is the man who cannot or will not admit their essential oneness, but pursues a separation that is no longer tenable. Thus, the speaker's concluding question, and the question ending "Embroidery (I)," is addressed not to herself but to her male partner. Each poem finishes with uncertainty about the "bridegroom," the man who must, it is implied, accept himself in a new way, just as the woman has come to a new understanding of herself. The questions at the end of the split-self poems have spoken to doubts and paradoxes in the female speaker. Now the queries shift to problems outside the self, where the unnatural, inhibiting conceptions still remain.

After the "Olga Poems," Levertov achieves peace with her split-selves. Their antagonism with each other no longer energizes poems, but the divided perspectives they represented still operate in the world. Increasingly, the split is found between the woman and the masculine-defined world, whether represented by the barbarism of war and urban terror, or the individual lover who is the spokesman for patriarchal values that would limit the woman in ways she once limited herself. This theme is found in Levertov's poems from the beginning, but reaches explicitness in two poems in *O Taste and See*—"The Ache of Marriage" and "About Marriage." It is hinted at in a third poem, "Losing Track." The isolation of the female speaker subjected to the gender expectations of the man underlies "The Cold Spring," "A Hunger," and "Adam's Complaint" in *Relearning the Alphabet*. The biographical denouement to this theme comes in the divorce poems of *The Freeing of the Dust*.

Recalling the concluding question of "The Wings"—"could I go / on one wing, / the white one?"—it is as if Levertov now realizes no flight is possible with only half her power. She must go on both wings, expending all her potential, black and white, just as she is both brides. Levertov was speaking about the dissociation of "humane responsibility" from "objective research" when she wrote the following passage, but it applies equally to the integrity of the self and the perversity of "shrinking to opposites": "Any human faculties and potentials that become divorced from the whole of which they are parts are . . . distorted. The compassionate imagination demands of us a wholeness and a constant interplay of functions. When we split ourselves up into opposing factions, fragments—intellect and emotions, body and spirit, private and public, etc.—we destroy ourselves."[8] From the early

8. Denise Levertov, "On 'The Malice of Innocence': Poetry in the Classroom," *American Poetry Review*, I (1972), 44.

poems, in which she feared and repressed her oppositions, to the poems in which she was able to admit their centrality but remain ambivalent and threatened, Levertov finally moves from split-selves to healed selves through acceptance and integration. "A Woman Alone," from her excellent collection *Life in the Forest* (1978), is a poem made possible by the resolution of the split-selves. In it Levertov celebrates the various aspects of her womanness and power without the guilt or fear present in earlier works.

> a kind of sober euphoria makes her believe
> in her future as an old woman, a wanderer,
> seamed and brown,
>
> . . . .
>
> an old winedrinking woman, who knows
> the old roads, grass-brown, and laughs to herself . . .
>
> . . . .
>
> . . . she thinks maybe
> she could get to be tough and wise, some way,
> anyway. Now at least
> she is past the time of mourning,
> now she can say without shame or deceit,
> O blessed Solitude.

Whole, self-assured, she stakes out a direction in which women grow wise and independent, moving into age with joy and inner beauty, even though—perhaps even because—men no longer figure centrally in their lives. As a poem of freedom and of women alone, it is a validation poem that points to new myths. Traditionally, as one critic has pointed out,

> the wise old man tells what experience has taught him, now too
> late to enjoy, then too quick to savor in fullness. The wise old
> woman, on the other hand, is generally wise by virtue of magic
> or herbal cookery. Her wisdom has been regarded as rather
> bogus or too supernatural to be dealt with. She has paid for it,
> like Cassandra, by her coupling with a god or devil. As she ages,
> like Snow White's step-mother, she approaches her mirror only

in shadows; and if the mirror speaks back, she candies an apple
with poison for the fair, young, and fertile.[9]

These myths of a "wise" woman regard her only in her relation to
men—her magic or insight effected by the supernatural agency of
men, or her actions prompted by fear of losing her sexual attractive-
ness, the only thing that makes her worthwhile. Levertov's speaker,
though she remembers men with pleasure, is not dominated by efforts
to please them; though she is surprised by age, she is graceful in handling it. Without apology, regret, or disguise, she is a woman who is
aging and alone, but who is also strong, wise, and laughing to herself.
Rather than "shrinking to opposites," she expresses a "sober euphoria"
of integrated, realized life and selfhood, celebrating possibilities and
"believ[ing] in her future as an old woman."

9. Richard Gustafson, "'Time Is a Waiting Woman': New Poetic Icons," *Midwest Quar-
terly*, XVI (1975), 318.

IV / What Does It Mean "To Survive"

THE POETRY OF ADRIENNE RICH

> What it means to be a man, what it means to be a woman, I think, is perhaps the major subject of poetry from here on. It's the ultimately political question, and it is going to affect all the other questions.
>
> **ADRIENNE RICH**

By the time Adrienne Rich's third book of poetry, *Snapshots of a Daughter-in-Law*, was published in 1963, praise of her earlier collections from such formidable critics as W. H. Auden, Randall Jarrell, and Donald Hall had firmly established her as a brilliant young poet and a stylist to be reckoned with. She was awarded the Yale Younger Poet's Prize in 1951 for her first book of poetry, *A Change of World*, and in 1955 she won the Ridgely Torrence Memorial Award for *The Diamond Cutters and Other Poems*.[1] She was married to a Harvard professor, had given birth to three sons, and seemed beyond question to have succeeded triumphantly in every conventional, and unconventional, area ascribed to women. But nearly nine years had passed between her second and third books. After *The Diamond Cutters* appeared, she wrote in her journal: "Of late I've felt toward poetry,—both reading and writing it—nothing but boredom and indifference. Especially toward my own work. . . . When I receive a letter soliciting mss., or someone alludes to my 'career,' I have a strong sense of wanting to deny all responsibility for and interest in that person who writes—or who wrote."[2] Rich speaks of herself as a poet in the past tense and seems to regard the idea of a writing career with irony. Something had happened, was happening. A poem written in the year *Snapshots* appeared after such long silence, speaks to the presence of strange and disturbing cataclysms in her life.

The Trees

The trees inside are moving out into the forest.

the forest that was empty all these days

1. References to the poems are from the following editions: *A Change of World* (New Haven, 1951); *The Diamond Cutters* (New York, 1955); *Snapshots of a Daughter-in-Law* (New York, 1966); *Leaflets* (New York, 1969); *The Will to Change* (New York, 1973); *Diving into the Wreck* (New York, 1973); *Poems Selected and New, 1950–1974* (New York, 1975); *The Dream of a Common Language* (New York, 1977).

2. Adrienne Rich, *Of Woman Born: Motherhood as Experience and Institution* (New York, 1976), 27. Hereinafter cited parenthetically in text as *OWB*.

where no bird could sit
no insect hide
no sun bury its feet in shadow
the forest that was empty all these nights
will be full of trees by morning.

All night the roots work
to disengage themselves from the cracks
in the veranda floor.
The leaves strain toward the glass
small twigs stiff with exertion
long-cramped boughs shuffling under the roof
like newly discharged patients
half-dazed, moving
to the clinic doors.

I sit inside, doors open to the veranda
writing long letters
in which I scarcely mention the departure
of the forest from the house.
The night is fresh, the whole moon shines
in a sky still open
the smell of leaves and lichen
still reaches like a voice into the rooms.
My head is full of whispers
which tomorrow will be silent.

Listen. The glass is breaking.
The trees are stumbling forward
into the night. Winds rush to meet them.
The moon is broken like a mirror,
its pieces flash now in the crown
of the tallest oak.

(1963)

From the perspective of women's isolation, particularly that of the
woman artist, it seems clear that Rich's subject is nothing less than the
diminution, indeed the wholesale decampment, of the vital imagination (the trees) that sustains creation, from the rigidity and limitations

of domestic enclosures (the house). Rich is describing, in terms that address both the landscape of the dream and the landscape of the mundane, the loss of her poetic powers. The trees have been "long-cramped," made "stiff" and weak by the strictures forced upon them, just as the woman has crippled her imaginative, poetic force by submitting it to the routine and limitations of a falsifying existence. Her tone and occupation, "writing long letters / in which I scarcely mention the departure / of the forest from the house," exemplify the loss of response and imagination that has already taken place. The most striking clash in the poem occurs in the third stanza, between the dramatic, powerful upheaval of the trees and the mundane activity of the woman, suggesting either that the reduction of her powers has been happening for some time and therefore is not 'news' or that she cannot acknowledge to herself or to others the extent of the damage, or both. All the sensual, visual appeals lie outside the boundaries of the house —the moonlight, the smell of leaves and lichen, the winds, and tall oaks—but the woman (perhaps fully dazed, as the trees are "half-dazed") passively remains inside where the forest reaches her "like a voice." Yet, as the movement of the trees and the poem forecasts, soon even this susceptibility to the imagination and its evocations will be gone. "My head is full of whispers / which tomorrow will be silent." The activity of the natural elements—trees stumbling, winds rushing—contrasts with the static, unresponding posture of the woman who stays isolated from them and from her own powers. Her reticence in the letters implies an isolation from others. The final image of a broken moon caught in the trees is her fragmented female self, now remote and inaccessible.

The poem bears a marked resemblance to Levertov's "The Dogwood," in which the retreat of the woman's creativity is signified by the distant lure of trees, the channeling of her energy into letters instead of poems, the presiding female presence of the moon, and a diffuse, distracted air in the face of compelling appeals from outside.

"The Trees" is obviously a poem in which many facets of isolation are embedded. Victimization is suggested by the enclosures and by the woman's efforts to deny what is happening, to not confront it with any power or resistance. There is also a split between inner and outer selves. For the moment, however, the victimization is qualified by the open door and the broken window, which figure strongly in the poem and which present at least the possibility of rebellion and escape. The relative position of doors—open or closed—and the intactness of glass are important indicators throughout Rich's poetry of the freedom and power allowed in the world of the poems. The significance of the open door and shattered glass in "The Trees" is apparent by contrast with the much earlier poem "Storm Warnings," from *A Change of World*, in which the scrupulously locked doors and shuttered windows cautioned against "weather in the heart." The message was withdrawal, reduction, and enclosure. Similarly, in "A View from the Terrace" and "The Uncle Speaks in the Drawing Room," the image of breaking glass is an emblem for the disruption of society; especially in the latter poem this is to be viewed with horror and alarm. In "The Middle-Aged," a poem from *The Diamond Cutters*, a crack in the windowpane alerts the speaker to the presence of secret pain and trauma in a superficially serene household.

By the time Rich is writing "The Trees," however, the force of imagination that has broken the glass asserts a heady freedom and momentum that will be the woman's if only she can pass through the door. The door leading out of the safe, but soon to be false and silent, room into the mystery and risk of the forest, represents the same boundary of irrevocable decision found in another poem about doors written a year earlier.

Prospective Immigrants Please Note

Either you will
go through this door
or you will not go through.

If you go through
there is always the risk
of remembering your name.

Things look at you doubly
and you must look back
and let them happen.

If you do not go through
it is possible
to live worthily

to maintain your attitudes
to hold your position
to die bravely

but much will blind you,
much will evade you,
at what cost who knows?

The door itself
makes no promises.
It is only a door.

1962

Clearly, to pass through the door is to change one's life forever. There can be no equivocation, no straddling of boundaries. On one side is safety, respectability, "attitudes" and "positions" but also the implication of illusion, evasion, and spiritual death. On the other side is the reality of self, but not without risk for those who have long harbored illusion. If one side is "blind," the other brings vision equally painful and the irrefutable status of an immigrant, a stranger, a pioneer in reality.

Surely some crisis is at hand. Windows are shattering, trees uprooting, moons breaking in the night, doors demanding the negotiations of some fearful rite of passage, while a woman writes innocuous letters mentioning none of these singularities. As a poet and as a woman, Rich can be said to have crossed the line she had drawn, but what had turned a safe, ordinary woman's room into a "clinic," a door into revelation?

Rich's first collection of poetry, *A Change of World*, was selected by W. H. Auden for the Yale Younger Poet's Prize in 1951, when Rich was a senior at Radcliffe. Auden's preface, paternal and patronizing, commending her for her "modesty," her good sense not to be original, and poems that "are neatly dressed, speak quietly," "don't tell fibs," and "respect their elders," has become an amusement to later critics, as well as an excellent example of sexist criticism. Yet Rich's poems *do* fit the description Auden gave them. By their own evidence and Rich's admission, they are strongly derivative of the male poetic giants of the first half of the twentieth century—Yeats, Frost, Eliot, Auden—with a chiseled precision and managed elegance of phrasing that, even in the

handling of modern pessimism and fragmentation, preserve a neat
decorum of thought and landscape. One critic has rightly suggested
that "what [Auden] heard in these poems was his own voice echoed
back to him, imitated by a schoolgirl for the approval of pedagogic and
paternal elders."[3] These early poems examine life on the safe side of
the door. The speakers "maintain their attitudes," "hold their positions," even "die bravely," but the continually disruptive current beneath the surface of Rich's technical brilliance and intellectual control
is the sense of evasion, the rumbling ominousness of the cost at which
safety is achieved. Despite the volume's title, safety seems predicated
on resistance to change, reduction in the scope of passion and imagination, enclosure of one's literal and psychic geography. The opening
poem of the volume, "Storm Warnings," gives the dominant tone of
Rich's passive, defensive posture.

> The glass has been falling all the afternoon,
> And knowing better than the instrument
> What winds are walking overhead, what zone
> Of gray unrest is moving across the land
> I leave the book upon a pillowed chair
> And walk from window to closed window, watching
> Boughs strain against the sky.
>
> And think again, as often when the air
> Moves inward toward a silent core of waiting,
> How with a single purpose time has traveled
> By secret currents of the undiscerned
> Into this polar realm. Weather abroad
> And weather in the heart alike come on
> Regardless of prediction.
>
> Between foreseeing and averting change
> Lies all the mastery of elements
> Which clocks and weatherglasses cannot alter.
> Time in the hand is not control of time,
> Nor shattered fragments of an instrument

3. Willard Spiegelman, "Voice of the Survivor: The Poetry of Adrienne Rich," *South-
west Review*, LX (1975), 372.

> A proof against the wind; the wind will rise,
> We can only close the shutters.

> I draw the curtains as the sky goes black
> And set a match to candles sheathed in glass
> Against the keyhole draught, the insistent whine
> Of weather through the unsealed aperture.
> This is our sole defense against the season;
> These are the things that we have learned to do
> Who live in troubled regions.

The "troubled regions" of *A Change of World* were the poet's struggles to live in the world as a woman. The view of Rich as a schoolgirl imitating male poets "for the approval of pedagogic and paternal elders" characterized not only her poetic practice but her private life as well. More than describing a woman poet he found congenial, Auden had furnished a précis of the type of woman a male society reinforced with its approbation. Making oneself small, passive, and sheltered was a way to handle the weather abroad and in the heart, but it was also the way to pass successfully as a feminine woman in Rich's time. At this point, the fact that passivity conflicted acutely with Rich's development and voice as a poet did not clearly emerge for her, but intuitively she felt that she could not be both a "successful" woman and a successful poet.

What is striking is the degree to which Rich's grasp of the conflict between successful femininity and successful artistry as a poet, though it was a vague, inchoate grasp, nevertheless emerged in the poems from the beginning. As Rich has pointed out, "Poems are like dreams, in them you put what you don't know you know."[4] The crisis that was building to conscious recognition in her life was already unconsciously feeding her poems. Thus, in *A Change of World*, a number of poems exemplify the emotional and physical landscape of women's isolation. "Storm Warnings" evokes the images and outlook of victimization in its stress on enclosure, emotional desolation, resistance to change and time, and the speaker's ultimate fear of loss of control. "Aunt Jennifer's

4. Adrienne Rich, "When We Dead Awaken: Writing as Re-vision," in Barbara Charlesworth Gelpi and Albert Gelpi (eds.), *Adrienne Rich's Poetry* (New York, 1975), 94.

Tigers," which follows "Storm Warnings," is an extension of this attitude toward the self and toward life. The fearful, gloomy woman waiting inside her darkening room for the emotional and meteorological
devastation to hit could be Aunt Jennifer, who is similarly passive and
terrified, overwhelmed by events that eclipsed her small strength.
"Aunt Jennifer's Tigers" is, however, an even clearer statement of conflict in women, specifically between the impulse to freedom and imagination (her tapestry of prancing tigers) and the "massive weight" of
gender roles and expectations, signified by "Uncle's wedding band."
Although separated through the use of the third person and a different generation, neither Aunt Jennifer in her ignorance nor Rich as a
poet recognizes the fundamental implications of the division between
imagination and duty, power and passivity. A companion to "Aunt
Jennifer's Tigers," the poem "Mathilde in Normandy" takes another
example of women's artistry in needlework as an expression of imagination and freedom that has no other outlet. Like the exotic panel of
tigers, the Bayeaux Tapestry produced by the noblewomen who were
kept at home ironically assumes an importance and power that eclipses
the actual lives of the men it depicts.

In a few early poems the life of independence and power attracts
the young woman, such as the speaker in "The Kursaal at Interlaken,"
who turns from the facile pleasantries and conventions of a man's
efforts to seduce her, to look at the solitary mountain peak: "Jungfrau,
the legendary virgin spire, / Consumes the mind with mingled snow
and fire." But more typical is the view presented in "An Unsaid Word."

> She who has the power to call her man
> From the estranged intensity
> Where his mind forages alone,
> Yet keeps her peace and leaves him free
> And when his thoughts to her return
> Stands where he left her, still his own,
> Knows this the hardest thing to learn.

In "Storm Warnings," "Aunt Jennifer's Tigers," "Mathilde in Normandy," and elsewhere, the woman's place is to be attendant, solicitous, unmoving, while the man ranges physically and intellectually in
the immensities of the world. Implicitly, she is second to the other de-

mands of his attention. There is no allowance for his standing in one place while her mind and person "forage alone." The final line almost explodes with understatement: "The hardest thing to learn." For Rich, it became impossible to learn, but at this point in her life she was still struggling with the forces confounding her lesson.

Rich had always learned her lessons well, and learned them primarily from men. Her early life was dominated by her father, a medical professor at Johns Hopkins University whom she described as "brilliant, ambitious, possessed by his own drive" and who, "like the transcendentalist Bronson Alcott, believed that he . . . could raise children according to his unique moral and intellectual plan" (*OWB*, 222). Precocious and intellectual herself, Rich strongly identified her early artistic efforts with her father. "For about twenty years I wrote for a particular man, who criticized and praised me and made me feel I was . . . 'special.' The obverse side of this, of course, was that I tried for a long time to please him, or rather, not to displease him."[5] A poem of Rich's, appropriately titled "Juvenalia," addresses this situation of the favorite daughter, who copies out her dutiful verses, her "praised and sedulous lines . . . for admiring friends / for you above all to read," while, ironically, the expensively bound copies of Ibsen's plays in her father's library rise in the cases above her, their message of rebellion and feminism lost on the small, local instance of conventional gender tyranny.

Later, at Radcliffe, there were more lessons to be learned from men.

> I went on to Radcliffe, congratulating myself that now I would
> have great men as my teachers. From 1947 to 1951, when I
> graduated, I never saw a single woman on a lecture platform,
> or in front of a class. . . . The 'great men' talked of other 'great
> men,' of the nature of Man, the history of Mankind, the future
> of man. . . . Women students simply were not taken very seri-
> ously. Harvard's message to women was an elite mystification:
> we were, of course, part of Mankind; we were special, achieving
> women . . . but of course our real goal was to marry—if pos-
> sible, a Harvard graduate.[6]

5. *Ibid.*, 93.
6. Adrienne Rich, "Taking Women Students Seriously," *On Lies, Secrets and Silence: Selected Prose 1966–1978* (New York, 1979), 238.

And always, for a young woman poet, there were the literary lessons.

> It seemed to be a given that men wrote poems and women fre-
> quently inhabited them. . . . I think it has been a peculiar con-
> fusion to the girl or woman who tries to write. . . . She goes to
> poetry or fiction for *her* way of being in the world, since she too
> has been putting words and images together; she is looking ea-
> gerly for guides, maps, possibilities; and over and over in the
> "words' masculine pervasive force" of literature she comes up
> against something that negates everything she is about: she
> meets the image of Woman in books written by men.[7]

There was tremendous pressure to *be* these images of women according to the standards of men, but they conflicted with "that absorbed,
drudging, puzzled, sometimes inspired creature . . . who sits at a desk
trying to put words together."[8] The irreconcilable messages from the
inner self and the outer world inevitably assumed the dimensions of
the split so frequent in the experience of women artists.

> To be "like other women" had been a problem for me. From the
> age of thirteen or fourteen, I had felt I was only acting the part
> of a feminine creature. At the age of sixteen my fingers were
> almost constantly ink-stained. The lipstick and high heels of the
> era were difficult-to-manage disguises. In 1945 I was writing po-
> etry seriously, and had a fantasy of going to postwar Europe as
> a journalist. . . . There were two different compartments, al-
> ready, to my life. But writing poetry, and my fantasies of travel
> and self-sufficiency, seemed more real to me; I felt that as an
> incipient "real woman" I was a fake. . . . This sense of acting a
> part created a curious sense of guilt, even though it was a part
> demanded for survival. (*OWB*, 25).

Instead of examining this split, this tension in her life, Rich, like
most women, blamed herself for her difference, her abnormality, and
found reassurance of her femininity in a marriage in 1953 to a Har-

---

7. Rich, "When We Dead Awaken," in Gelpi and Gelpi (eds.), *Adrienne Rich's Poetry*,
93–94.
8. *Ibid.*, 94.

vard graduate and professor of economics, Alfred Conrad.[9] Soon after, when she was expecting their first child, Rich wrote, "As soon as I was visibly and clearly pregnant, I felt, for the first time in my adolescent and adult life, not guilty" (*OWB*, 26).

Although Rich had published *The Diamond Cutters* to critical acclaim in 1955 and was emerging as a young poet of considerable potential, the circumstances of life as wife and mother in academic Cambridge, and the constant care of small children (Rich gave birth to three sons in four years: 1955, 1957, and 1959), resulted in the attrition of her practical and spiritual powers. Already, the poems in *The Diamond Cutters* project a sad, grim sense of living in a world where it is too late for peace and simplicities. Throughout the nostalgic conceits is woven a dominant mood of darkness and fatality. The poems in which the speaker assumes the perspective of an alien are based largely on Rich's feelings as a woman searching for her identity in a world defined by males. In many of the poems, the predominant image of a train rushing without a destination evokes repeatedly the sense of helplessness and entrapment, of being hurled into the unknown with little control or knowledge, a characteristic response to victimization. Perhaps Rich's own immediate experience comes closest to the surface in the long narrative portraits of the middle section, "Autumn Equinox" and "The Perennial Answer." Both poems concern the emotional desolation of women locked in regrettable marriages and roles. "Autumn Equinox" describes a marriage which resembles that of a Dorothea Brooke to a Dr. Casaubon. A woman is first attracted to a man because he shares her intellectual interests—interests that set the woman apart from other women.

> Reading too much, sneering at other girls
> Whose learning was of cookery and flirtation.
> Father would have me clever, sometimes said
> He'd let me train for medicine, like a son,
> To come into his practice. So I studied
> German and botany . . .

9. Alfred H. Conrad was a graduate student and had been previously married when Rich met him. His doctoral work was on the institution of slavery. He committed suicide in 1970.

It is her husband, however, who goes on to lead the life she had glimpsed, while she learns through the years to subordinate her strengths to his. Her only outlet of defiance is to hang gaudy curtains that shock the staid, academic village. Unhappy, trapped, disliking her life but without precedent for articulating her grievances, she wakes distraught in the night and can only explain herself with the lame, "I'm sick, I guess— / I thought that life was different than it is."

In "The Snow Queen," Rich pictures herself as both the cold, proud artist (the snow queen) and the human who has caught a splinter of glass in her eye (her desire to be an artist), causing the world to look ugly and distorted according to the Hans Christian Andersen story. Her guilts emerge in the association of her artistic self with forces that deny love and solicitude to others, though she is attracted to the solitary, cold, authoritative figure of the queen. It is a split-self poem with many images similar to those of Levertov.

Most of the poems in *The Diamond Cutters* had been written much earlier than the 1956 publication date, and little in Rich's life encouraged or allowed her to do more. It was taken for granted that her husband's profession was the one the family supported. "*His* work, *his* professional life, was the real work in the family; in fact, this was for years not even an issue between us. I understood that my struggles as a writer were a kind of luxury, a peculiarity of mine. . . . I experienced my depressions, bursts of anger, sense of entrapment, as burdens my husband was forced to bear because he loved me; I felt grateful to be loved in spite of bringing him those burdens" (*OWB*, 27). Even her legitimate anger against the limitations of her creativity and personal struggles for identity Rich felt as guilts and abnormalities. "I had a marriage and a child. If there were doubts, if there were periods of dull depression or active despairing, these could only mean that I was ungrateful, insatiable, perhaps a monster."[10] The other examples of feminine behavior in her life only intensified her unrest. With hindsight, she describes the daily rhythms of women's lives around her. "The life of a Cambridge tenement backyard swarming with children, the repetitious cycles of laundry, the nightwakings, the interrupted

10. Rich, "When We Dead Awaken," in Gelpi and Gelpi (eds.), *Adrienne Rich's Poetry*, 95.

moments of peace or of engagement with ideas, the ludicrous dinner parties at which young wives, some with advanced degrees, all seriously and intelligently dedicated to their children's welfare and their husband's careers, attempted to reproduce the amenities of Brahmin Boston, amid French recipes and the pretense of effortlessness— above all, the ultimate lack of seriousness with which women were regarded in that world—all of this defied analysis" (*OWB*, 27).

Rich knew finally, irrevocably, "I had to remake my own life" (*OWB*, 27). She has written that "about the time my third child was born, I felt that I had either to consider myself a failed woman and failed poet, or to try to find some synthesis by which to understand what was happening to me. . . . What I did write was unconvincing to me; my anger and frustration were hard to acknowledge in or out of poems."[11]

Rich intuitively rejected much of her writing, some almost as soon as it was written. Of *A Change of World*, she recalls, "There were a lot of poems I couldn't write even, because I didn't want to confess to having that much aggression, that much ego, that much sense of myself. I had always thought of my first book as being a book of very well-tooled poems by a sort of very bright student."[12] She felt it had been published only by a "fluke." Although *The Diamond Cutters and Other Poems* won her additional commendations, Rich admits, "By the time it came out I was already dissatisfied with those poems, which seemed to me mere exercises for the poems I hadn't written."[13] She stated further, "I really wouldn't have published [it] except that I needed to publish a second book—much of it was filled with verse exercises showing how well I could do what I knew I could do well, how I could do it in 'their' [male] terms, how I could do it as well as Richard Wilbur or various other people. That was the most praised book I published for many years, although I *knew* it was not what it should have been, what I wanted it to be."[14] Rich had written in her journal soon after *The Dia-*

---

11. *Ibid.*
12. Stanley Plumly, Wayne Dodd, and Walter Trevis, "Talking with Adrienne Rich," *Ohio Review*, XIII (1971), 31.
13. Rich, "When We Dead Awaken," in Gelpi and Gelpi (eds.), *Adrienne Rich's Poetry*, 95.
14. "Adrienne Rich and Robin Morgan Talk About Poetry and Women's Culture," in Kirsten Grimstad and Susan Rennie (eds.), *New Women's Survival Sourcebook* (New York, 1975), 107.

mond Cutters appeared, "If there is going to be a real break in my writing life, this is as good a time for it as any. I have been dissatisfied with myself, my work, for a long time" (*OWB*, 27).

II

Part of Rich's dissatisfaction with her work came from her own knowledge of how much she was guarding, distorting, and altering her work to accommodate some external standard of appropriate literary material and form. Much of the subject matter emerging from her female experience was recast or outcast altogether. "Afterward," "The Tourist and the Town," "Antinous: The Diaries," and "The Loser," are among the poems in which personae were changed to indicate male speakers, though the participants and their sensibilities were without question manifestations of Rich herself. The meaning of the poems shifts considerably when this change is acknowledged. Rich altered poems to avoid confronting her own inner conflicts, as in "Stepping Backward," which reads as a love poem to a man. The poem was based, however, on a relationship between Rich and another woman.[15] Through the act of a formal farewell, the intellectualizing of the emotions, the misleading gender, Rich evades her true feelings. The poem asks, "How far dare we throw off the daily ruse, / Official treacheries of face and name, / Have out our true identity?" and Rich's answer is to step backward, to literally retreat from self-discovery and "true identity." Later poems like "To Judith, Taking Leave," were never published at all when they were written. As Rich had formulated the crisis to herself, she had either to accept failure as a woman and a poet or to find a new synthesis that would allow her to express her sense of how those two aspects of herself were inextricably linked. She could not be

15. Rich said of this poem: "It's about acknowledging one's true feelings to another person; it's a very guarded, carefully-wrought poem. It's in the form of a farewell, but a farewell which was taken in order to step backward and look at the person more clearly, which makes it safer to look at the relationship, because it's as if you were saying goodbye. That poem is addressed to a woman whom I was close to in my late teens, and whom I really fled from—I fled from my feelings about her. It's very intellectualized, but it's really the first poem in which I was striving to come to terms with feelings for women." Elly Bulkin, "An Interview with Adrienne Rich," *Conditions: One* (1977), 50.

the poet she felt she could be unless she stopped divorcing her art from the literal and psychic lifeblood of her existence.

Energy and conviction for new work were returning after indifference to past accomplishments. She wrote in her journal in June, 1958, "The work that is before me is serious and difficult and not at all clear even as to plan. Discipline of mind and spirit, uniqueness of expression, ordering of daily existence, the most effective functioning of the human self—these are the chief things I wish to achieve" (*OWB*, 28). Two months later, just at the point where her time and life were becoming her own, she was set back by the news she was pregnant with her third child. She realized that her hard-won creative redirection would be postponed, but she determined it would not be killed off. In a journal entry of August, 1958, she is both poignant and tough.

> I have to acknowledge to myself that I would not have chosen
> to have more children, that I was beginning to look to a time,
> not too far off, when I should again be free, no longer so physi-
> cally tired. . . . The *only* way I can develop now is through
> much harder, more continuous, connected work than my pres-
> ent life makes possible. Another child means postponing this
> for some years longer—and years at my age are significant, not
> to be tossed lightly away. . . . If more effort has to be made then
> I will make it. If more despair has to be lived through, I think I
> can anticipate it correctly and live through it. (*OWB*, 28–9)

Snapshots of a Daughter-in-Law (1963) was the result of Rich's rededication to poetry and to the truth of her life. In parts of this transitional book, Rich retains her accustomed techniques and means of treatment, while in other parts she takes risks with new material and new forms. The collection, as one critic notes, "begins in one place and ends in another." There is still evidence of "the gifted ventriloquism" that had characterized *A Change of World* and *The Diamond Cutters*, but by the middle of the book, with the edgy, brilliant title poem, "her themes—the burden of history, the separateness of individuals, the need for relationships where there is no other transcendence—begin to find their clarifying focus and center: that she is a woman and poet in late twentieth century America.[16] It was also in this volume that Rich began her practice, which has continued, of dating her poems in an effort to link them more firmly to the rhythms of her life, to claim a personal and temporal validity for them, as one would for diary or journal entries.

Several early poems in the book confess to the collapse of old assumptions about the world, for example, "From Morning-Glory to Petersburg (*The World Book*, 1928)."

> I can recall when knowledge still was pure,
>   not contradictory, pleasurable
>   as cutting out a paperdoll.
> You opened up a book and there it was:
>   everything just as promised
>
> . . . .
>   . . . Now knowledge finds me out;
>   in all its risible untidiness
>   it traces me to each new address,
> dragging in things I never thought about.
>
> . . . .
>   . . . a family
> of jeering irresponsibles always
>   comes along gypsy-style
>   and there you have them all
> forever on your hands. It never pays.

Her jibe is clearly at the pretensions of books and scientific facts to contain the world. The focus of knowledge shifts from analytic, printed facts to the messier but more accurate basis of human experience, from *The World Book* to the family of gypsies. Although it is subliminal here, Rich will eventually pursue this distinction between ways of knowing as a basic differentiation between masculine and feminine forms of perception, roughly dividing between objective and subjective sensibilities, with the former tending, in her belief, to falsify life.

This new, disorderly basis for knowledge presents difficulties with

16. Albert Gelpi, "Adrienne Rich: The Poetics of Change," in Robert B. Shaw (ed.), *American Poetry Since 1960: Some Critical Perspectives* (London, 1973), 126–27.

the literary forms that must contain such ragged and stubborn reality,
a realization reached in the poem following "From Morning-Glory to
Petersburg." "Rural Reflections" states the problem.

> This is the grass your feet are planted on.
> You paint it orange or you sing it green,
>   But you have never found
> A way to make the grass mean what you mean.
>
> .   .   .   .
>
> It is the grass that cuts the mower down;
> It is the cloud that swallows up the sky.

The germinal title poem, "Snapshots of a Daughter-in-Law," was
written over a period of several years. Its curt, irregular form and its
patching of letters, quotes, personae, and moods, accurately reflect the
fluctuations in a woman's daily spiritual and practical life. As the title
implies, it is a series of still-life images of women in their various legal,
emotional, and social relations to men; inevitably, it is also about their
relationship or, more accurately, their lack of relationship to other
women.

> You, once a belle in Shreveport,
> with henna-colored hair, skin like a peach bud.
> Still have your dresses copied from that time,
> and play a Chopin prelude
> called by Cortot: "Delicious recollections
> float like perfume through the memory."
>
> Your mind now, mouldering like wedding-cake,
> heavy with useless experience, rich
> with suspicion, rumor, fantasy,
> crumbling to pieces under the knife-edge
> of mere fact. In the prime of your life.
>
> Nervy, glowering, your daughter
> wipes the teaspoons, grows another way.

Their roles as sexual adjuncts to men divide them from their powers
and abilities, turn them to divisive competition with, and suspicion of,

other women, and lock their sense of self-worth into an endless play
for male approval, to the detriment of their minds,

> A thinking woman sleeps with monsters.
> The beak that grips her, she becomes.

of their bodies,

> *Dulce ridens, dulce loquens,*
> she shaves her legs until they gleam
> like petrified mammoth-tusk.

and of their spirits,

> Sometimes she's let the tapstream scald her arm,
> a match burn to her thumbnail,
>
> or held her hand above the kettle's snout
> right in the wooly steam.
> . . . nothing hurts her any more, except
> each morning's grit blowing into her eyes.

Numbed by the narrowness of her intellectual and emotional life,
driven half-mad by the attrition of her possibilities, a woman thinks
she hears voices urging her to violent, egotistical acts.

> Only a week since They said: *Have no patience.*
>
> The next time it was: *Be insatiable.*
> Then: *Save yourself; others you cannot save.*

Yet when anger is allowed to escape, it is inevitably directed against
other women. Wit turns to rancor and energy turns to destruction,
with each woman dragging the other down. Rather than confronting
their real enemy, they become fellow victims.

> Two handsome women, gripped in argument,
> each proud, acute, subtle, I hear scream
> across the cut glass and majolica
> like Furies cornered from their prey:
> The argument *ad feminam,* all the old knives
> that have rusted in my back, I drive in yours,
> *ma semblable, ma soeur!*

The isolation of women from women curses each to repeat the ancient failures.

Containing no vision of women's real possibilities is the conception men have created and held them to.

> When to her lute Corinna sings
> neither words nor music are her own;
> only the long hair dipping
> over her cheek, only the song
> of silk against her knees
> and these
> adjusted in reflections of an eye

Rich nevertheless chastises women for failing to seize the moment of their ambitions and desires, laments their collusion in the crippling of life's chances, and as befits a poet, focuses on the distortions that continue to appear in their writing.

> Deliciously, all that we might have been
> all that we were—fire, tears,
> wit, taste, martyred ambition—
> stirs like the memory of refused adultery
> the drained and flagging bosom of our middle years.

> *Not that it is done well, but*
> *that it is done at all?* Yes, think
> of the odds! or shrug them off forever.
> This luxury of the precocious child,
> Time's precious chronic invalid,—
> would we, darlings, resign it if we could?
> Our blight has been our sinecure:
> mere talent was enough for us—
> glitter in fragments and rough drafts.

> .   .   .   .

> Bemused by gallantry, we hear
> our mediocrities over-praised,
> indolence read as abnegation,
> slattern thought styled intuition,
> every lapse forgiven, our crime

only to cast too bold a shadow
or smash the mould right off.

Rich envisions a beautiful woman—part bird, part helicopter—a
sacrificial figure "more merciless to herself than history," who will dare
the "solitary confinement, / tear gas, attrition shelling," the full resistance of a society whose fundamental human delineation and patterns
she overturns. Rich is a long way from seeing herself in this role of
liberator and prophet, and even felt, after writing "Snapshots," that
she had still been distancing herself from the rage and rebellion of the
poem through liberal use of literary allusion, authorial commentary,
and third-person references to women. Nevertheless, "I was able to
write, for the first time, directly about experiencing myself as a woman.
. . . It was an extraordinary relief to write that poem."[17] Rich moves
from the victimization in her early poems, which expressed itself in the
prevalence of negative enclosures, emotional morbidity, resistance to
change and time, and abandonment of control, to a point of personalization in her handling of the isolation of women. From encoding and
retreat, she breaks through to confrontation and a new willingness to
speak the painful truth of her everyday experience as a woman.

As Rich discovers, in the complex, perfectly achieved "Double
Monologue," to address relationships with new honesty is no longer to
be able to "live illusionless, in the abandoned mine- / shaft of doubt,
and still / mine illusions for others," a reference to her earlier poetry
of brilliant surfaces and willed conclusions. She is on a quest for truth,
even though "truth no longer seems the most beautiful of words," and
she recognizes that in a world where all the truths are to be found
again, "our need mocks our gear." Even when the truths have been
arduously mined, the transference of knowledge is prone to defeat
and misinterpretation. The inadequacy of words, the isolation determined by all the insurmountable differences in the language spoken
by women and by men, intensifies through each successive book of
Rich's, becoming in time her dominant theme. In *Snapshots* it appears
in the poems that explore what one critic has called "the silent isolation

17. Rich, "When We Dead Awaken," in Gelpi and Gelpi (eds.), *Adrienne Rich's Poetry*, 97.

of minds in marriage."[18] Thus, in "A Marriage in the Sixties," Rich suc-cinctly raises and defeats the hope of essential communication.

> Two strangers, thrust for life upon a rock,
> may have at last the perfect hour of talk
> that language aches for; still—
> two minds, two messages.

In "The Lag," Rich uses the temporal phenomenon of jet lag as a metaphor for her advanced perceptions about gender relations; but her efforts to reach her male companion with what she knows cannot bridge the disparity in their conceptions, and the man remains literally and figuratively in the dark.[19]

> With you it is still the middle of the night.
> Nothing I know will make you know
> what birds cried me awake
> or how the wet light leaked
> into my sky.
>
> . . . .
>
> I'm older now than you.
> I feel your black dreams struggling at a porthole
> stuffed full of night, I feel you choking
> in that thick place. My words
> reach you as through a telephone
> where some submarine echo of my voice
> blurts knowledge you can't use.
>
> 1962

Closely connected to the perspective of "The Lag" is the poem "Ghost of a Chance."

> You see a man
> trying to think

---

18. Helen Vendler, "Ghostlier Demarcations, Keener Sounds," in Gelpi and Gelpi (eds.), *Adrienne Rich's Poetry*, 165.

19. "The Lag" appeared in the original *Snapshots*, but was not included in the 1967 Norton reprint. Several other changes were made in this volume: "The Classmate" was

You want to say
to everything:
Keep off! Give him room!
But you only watch,
terrified
the old consolations
will get him at last
like a fish
half-dead from flopping
and almost crawling
across the shingle,
almost breathing
the raw, agonizing
air
till a wave
pulls it back blind into the triumphant
sea.

1962

The poem bears an interesting comparison to "An Unsaid Word" in *A Change of World* as an index to the transformation Rich has undergone. Both poems focus on the efforts of a man to think, but the power balance has shifted completely. In the former, the man is a quester on the boundaries of knowledge, foraging alone with "estranged intensity," while the woman observes him with admiration and respect; her mark of esteem lies in her ability to preserve the familiar, comfortable world upon his return. In the latter, it is the woman who has surpassed the man in awareness and intellectual power. To push the boundaries of thought is no longer the solitary luxury of one man; it has become the evolutionary imperative of the race. The sight of the man thinking has become something painful and terrifying for the woman, who must witness the struggle to surmount "the old consolations," the old self-serving masculine patterns of perception. Just as in "Prospective Immigrants Please Note" and "The Lag," the woman has passed an irre-

---

dropped and a poem titled "The Likeness" was added; a poem originally titled "Well in a Ruined Courtyard" was retitled "The Well."

vocable boundary, but she seems powerless to provide transit for the
man, who must cross for himself. The telephone line goes dead, the
fish gasps back into the sea, and the story of men and women remains
"two minds, two messages."[20]

The final poem of *Snapshots* is "The Roofwalker," dedicated to
Denise Levertov.[21] In this moving, exhilarating, cautionary poem, Rich
at last abandons enclosures, the conventional "blueprints" of women's
lives, abandons the grating intimacy of the "old consolations," and sets
off with heady freedom, alone, to go beyond lives she can no longer
live in.

> Over the half-finished houses
> night comes. The builders
> stand on the roof. It is
> quiet after the hammers,
> the pulleys hang slack.
> Giants, the roofwalkers,
> on a listing deck, the wave
> of darkness about to break
> on their heads. The sky
> is a torn sail where figures
> pass magnified, shadows
> on a burning deck.
>
> I feel like them up there:
> exposed, larger than life,
> and due to break my neck.
>
> Was it worthwhile to lay—
> with infinite exertion—
> a roof I can't live under?

20. In her review of Mary Daly's *Beyond God the Father*, Rich wrote, "Women and men
who have gone through even limited painful recognitions in their personal lives, who
have courageously worked their way into a new perception of private reality, know what
kinds of seduction and threat the psyche can marshal against the process. When the
struggle is no longer confined to individual 'problems' but expands into the wider struggle to rethink the entire relation of the sexes in the hope of beginning to create a new
kind of human being, the structure of civilization seems poised to disarm us." In *Washing-
ton Post Book World*, November 11, 1973, p. 2.
21. It was Denise Levertov, as reader for Norton, who convinced them to publish
Adrienne Rich.

> —All those blueprints,
> closing of gaps,
> measurings, calculations?
> A life I didn't choose
> chose me: even
> my tools are the wrong ones
> for what I have to do.
> I'm naked, ignorant,
> a naked man fleeing
> across the roofs,
> who could with a shade of difference
> be sitting in the lamplight
> against the cream wallpaper
> reading—not with indifference—
> about a naked man
> fleeing across the roofs.

The poem is a culmination and a beginning of the various movements in *Snapshots*. Rich is escaping from a life that had become false to her art and experience: "A life I didn't choose / chose me." The "measurings, calculations" might well include allusion to her apprenticeship in a highly formalized, perfectionist poetic style; as she notes, "even / my tools are the wrong ones / for what I have to do." Her earlier poetics, no less than her patriarchal education, have made her lamentably unfit for the new work that lies before her: the articulation of feminine experience. Naked and ignorant, without inner or outer trappings of the life she had had no choice in and without the blueprints that built nothing she could use, she flees into a risky, committed freedom.

If Adrienne Rich had felt "due to break [her] neck" in her new personal and poetic stance, her fear seemed to materialize in critical reaction to *Snapshots*. Years later, she spoke of her own risk in the book and the effect of critical opinion about it.

> The book . . . *Snapshots of a Daughter-in-Law*, in which I was
> changing my forms, changing my structures, writing about
> women's lives, writing about my own life directly and nakedly
> for that time and for me at that time—this book was ignored,

was written off as being too bitter and personal. Yet I *knew* I
had gone out beyond in that book. I was also very conscious of
male critics, then, and it was like flunking a course. It was as
though they were telling me, "You did do well in book two, but
you flunked in book three." But I *knew* I was stronger as a poet,
I knew I was stronger in my connection with myself.[22]

It is interesting that Rich turns instinctively to that hoary male power
constellation of teacher and woman student to describe her response
to the dismissal her work met with, for, as a poet, she had been a student all along. To step out of that dutiful, ventriloquistic relation and
assert her own authority was to "flunk."

Rich's reaction was not so much to turn back from the momentum
of her new course as to hold it in abeyance.

I certainly didn't abandon the new forms I have developed, and
I *couldn't* retreat from female themes, but I did retreat from
dealing with them as openly as I had in *Snapshots*. And I also
became focused on the theme of death, which certainly was not
mere coincidence. It was as though something in me was saying,
"If my material, my subject matter as a woman is going to be
denied me, then there is only *one* other subject for me and that
is death." That's why *Necessities of Life* is a book about death.[23]

The use of death themes to encode women's anger and sense of lost
identity is a compelling amalgam, certainly verifiable in the poetry of
Louise Bogan, Sylvia Plath, and Diane Wakoski. But there is evidence
in *Necessities of Life* (1966) that Rich's energy has not been diverted entirely from its source. The opening, and title, poem of the volume re-
capitulates her tenacious efforts to carve an identity for herself from
the welter of personal, literary, childhood, and adolescent influences,
and against the sometimes enslaving pull of others. The indefatigable
efforts to name herself and to introduce herself into the world on her
own terms represent the essential task, "the bare necessities," and
"Soon / practice may make me middling perfect, I'll dare inhabit the

22. Grimstad and Rennie, *Sourcebook*, 107.
23. *Ibid*.

world." The poem concludes with the optimistic movement out and upward.

> I have invitations:
> a curl of mist streams upward
>
> from a field, visible as my breath,
> houses along a road stand waiting
>
> like old women, knitting, breathless
> to tell their tales.

In an interesting shift from "The Roofwalker," the houses are no longer only full of indifferent observers, but of women anxious to "tell their tales" to the one they recognize can give them "breath."

The inclusion of "The Trees" (discussed earlier) in the collection is an expression of Rich's fears that negative critical reaction would cut her off from her true poetic material. The theme of failed communication between men and women receives wry treatment in "Two Songs," in which the female speaker understands the man's language only because she has "picked it up in cultural exchanges." While their physical bodies momentarily relate, her wry *"Spasibo. Thanks. OK."* makes their verbal efforts strange. In a more serious, complex treatment, "Like This Together," dedicated to her husband, again commonalities of a household, a past, a day-to-day relation bind the couple in an intimacy that passes for marital fulfillment but that the speaker associates with a parked car and the couple in it, "sitting like drugged birds in a case." She gives the keynote of their relation—"Our words misunderstood us"—so that only a perpetual "fierce attention / gets hyacinths out of those / hard cerebral lumps."

A strong poem, "Night Pieces: For a Child," explores the dark, terrifying possibility that fear and alienation between the sexes is perhaps innate and insuperable. The speaker, a mother going to her young son's crib to adjust the cover, stirs him awake by mistake, only to witness his terror at her face.

> Your eyes
> spring open, still filmed in dream.
> Wider, they fix me—
> —death's head, sphinx, medusa?

> You scream.
> Tears lick my cheeks, my knees
> droop at your fear.
> Mother I no more am
> but woman, and nightmare.

Her heart breaks as she wonders what ancient embedded image the male apprehends in her sex which blasts her solicitous act of love. Her recognition is akin to that revealed in "The Knot."

> In the heart of the queen anne's lace, a knot of blood.
> For years I never saw it,
>
> . . . .
>
> and there, all along, the tiny dark-red spider
> sitting in the whiteness of the bridal web,
>
> waiting to plunge his crimson knifepoint
> into the white apparencies.
>
> Little wonder the eye, healing, sees
> for a long time through a mist of blood.

At the heart of the most intimate gender relationships is a knot of blood, a spider waiting in the bridal web, the illusion-seeking eye that for years does not comprehend the sacrifice, the mist of blood that maintains the heart intact.

III

Rich may have felt she was undercutting her female themes in *Necessities*, but she was never again to look back. By the time *Leaflets* was published in 1969, her imperative for the truth of all human relations—sexual, social, economic, and emotional—fused in a political vision and commitment that has radicalized with every subsequent collection. In a study of the treatment of isolation and its manifestations in different themes, *Leaflets* is interesting for its number of split-self poems, following the victimization poems of her early work and the personalization poems she turned to in *Snapshots*. Her previous collections have included examples of split-self delineations, such as "The Tree" in *The Diamond Cutters* and "Antinous: The Diaries" in *Snapshots*, but these do not have the sense of intention found in Levertov's split-self poems or in her own "Orion," "5:30 A.M.," "Abnegation," and "Women," in *Leaflets*.

"Orion" is an appeal to the cold, remote, starry power for an "old transfusion" of purpose and ambition that the woman speaker prefers to project onto the constellation rather than admit is truly her own.

> Far back when I went zig-zagging
> through tamarack pastures
> you were my genius, you
> my cast-iron Viking, my helmed
> lion-heart king in prison.
> . . . my fierce half-brother,
>
> . . . .
>
> as I throw back my head to take you in
> an old transfusion happens again:
> divine astronomy is nothing to it.

"Orion" is a split-self poem in which Rich's artistic nature, with its attendant qualities of egotism, independence, and power, is projected onto the male constellation. Like Levertov, the artist self is split off precisely because it conflicts with the approved exemplification of femininity and women's roles; hence, it is often cast in masculine form or as a socially peripheral female. Also, it is necessary to see the aberrant qualities as "bad."

> The poem "Orion" . . . is a poem of connection with a part of myself I had felt I was losing—the active principle, the energetic imagination, the "half-brother" whom I projected, as I had for many years, into the constellation Orion. It's no accident that the words "cold and egotistical" appear in this poem and are applied to myself. The choice still seemed to be between "love"—womanly, maternal love, altruistic love, a love defined and ruled by the weight of an entire culture; and egotism—a force directed by men into creation, achievement, ambition.[24]

24. Rich, "When We Dead Awaken," in Gelpi and Gelpi (eds.), *Adrienne Rich's Poetry*, 97.

The familiar divisions of split-selves appear in the poem—the contrast between the inner world of domestic enclosures and the outer world of freedom and action, between a poisoning emotional claustrophobia and what may be an equally poisoning emotional isolation.

> Indoors I bruise and blunder,
> break faith, leave ill enough
> alone,
>
> . . . .
>
> A man reaches behind my eyes
> and finds them empty
> a woman's head turns away
> from my head in the mirror
> children are dying my death
> and eating crumbs of my life.
>
> Pity is not your forte.
> Calmly you ache up there
>
> . . . .
>
> and when I look you back
>
> it's with a starlike eye
> shooting its cold and egotistical spear
> where it can do least damage.
> Breathe deep! No hurt, no pardon
> out here in the cold with you
> you with your back to the wall.

In April, 1965, Rich wrote of the struggle going on in her life.

Anger, weariness, demoralization. Sudden bouts of weeping. A sense of insufficiency to the moment and to eternity. . . . Paralyzed by the sense that there exists a mesh of relations between *e.g.* my rejection and anger at [her children], my sensual life, pacifism, sex (I mean in its broadest significance, not merely physical desire)—an interconnectedness which, if I could see it, make it valid, would give me back myself, make it possible to function lucidly and passionately—Yet I grope in and out among these dark webs— (*OWB*, 30)

In the second half of *Leaflets*, the "connectedness" Rich had been searching for between her physical and psychic life and the physical and psychic life of her time achieves lucidity and passion in the assault against patriarchal domination. The book moves with rising energy and power toward the final, iconoclastic title poem and the "ghazals." Ghazals are poems based on forms devised by the mid-nineteenth-century Urdu poet, Mirza Ghalib. They appealed to Rich for the fluidity and resonance achievable with the floating couplets, which she viewed as a form particularly suited to evoking what she calls "an age of political and cultural break-up."[25] These poems are written from the energy and despair of the political upheavals against the industrial military complex (during the 1960s) and the oppression of minorities, which fused for Rich with the sexual oppression she had increasingly articulated. ("Did you think I was talking about my life? / I was trying to drive a tradition up the wall.") She seems capable of nothing less than revolution in these poems about altering the private and public dehumanizations wrought by a male-controlled world gone amok. For Rich, the military and ecological rape of the earth bears every connection to the rape and dehumanization of women; the distortion of male power is perpetuated only through the distortion of female powerlessness. As she asserts in an essay exploring rape and war,

> For centuries the patriarchy has maintained itself by asking
> what was good for males, has assumed male norms and values
> as universal ones, has allowed the differences of "otherness,"
> the division of male and female consciousness, to become a ter-
> rifying dissociation of sensibility. The idea of woman exists at a
> strangely primitive level in the male psyche. She remains, for all
> his psychological self-consciousness, the object-figure on which
> can be projected all that man does not understand, all that he
> needs, all that he dreads, in his own experience. . . . Denying
> his own feminine aspects, always associating his manhood with
> his ability to possess and dominate women, man the patriarch
> has slowly, imperceptibly, over time, achieved a degree of self-
> estrangement, self-hatred and self-mutilation which is coming

25. Rich, *Leaflets*, 59.

to have almost irreversible effects on human relationships and
on the natural world.[26]

The struggle against this distortion cannot be too desperate; no old
view of the world can be left safe. She concludes "On Edges" with a
testament of her preparedness for risk and pain.

> I'd rather
> taste blood, yours or mine, flowing
> from a sudden slash, than cut all day
> with blunt scissors on dotted lines
> like the teacher told.

In "Leaflets" she avows that "life without caution" is "the only worth
living."

Her poems assume new urgency; as the title suggests, they are leaflets passed out from the front lines of a war being fought against an
enemy whose "constitution" is to "Obey the little laws and break the
great ones," to obey the insignificant, man-made laws and transgress
the laws of the human spirit. Her poems speak with the pain, passion,
and flux of their time.

> I want to hand you this
> leaflet streaming with rain or tears
> but the words coming clear
> something you might find crushed in your hand
> after passing a barricade
> and stuff in your raincoat pocket.

She asks simply, with the awareness of the outsider, the furtive resister,
"What else does it come down to / but handing on scraps of paper . . .
because the imagination crouches in them."

At the same time she is buoyed by the glimpses of change and the
possibilities for pioneering in new modes of human existence.

> From here on, all of us will be living
> like Galileo turning his first tube at the stars.
> ("8/8/68: i")

26. Adrienne Rich, "Caryatid: A Column," *American Poetry Review* (May–June,
1973), 10.

> I am thinking how we can use what we have
> to invent what we need.
> ("Leaflets")

"Invent what we need"—what is needed is nothing less than new myths. As Rich understands it, "A myth is not something that springs 'clean and clear' out of the imagination . . . but is rather a response to the environment, an interaction between the mind and its external world. It expresses a need, a longing. And myth has always accumulated, accreted; the profile of the goddess or the hero is always changing, weathered by changes in external conditions" (*OWB*, 92). Having fused sexual and political themes in *Leaflets*, Rich, in her subsequent collections—*The Will to Change* (1971), *Diving into the Wreck* (1973), and *The Dream of a Common Language* (1977)—continues to write poems exploring the old sexual divisions. Scenes of literal and psychic battle recapitulate the destructive isolation of women from men, women from women, and women from themselves. More compelling is a fundamental movement toward a repossessing, a renaming, a fresh view of the truths and possibilities of women's lives in a way that transfigures past archetypes and gives rise to new prototypes of women. Rich's metaphor for what she has undertaken is "diving into the wreck," the title of the volume for which she won the National Book Award in 1974 (an award she refused at first but later accepted in the name of all women whose voices have been lost or silenced). The wreck represents the battered hulk of the sexual definitions of the past, which Rich, as an underwater explorer, must search for evidence of what can be salvaged. Only those who have managed to survive the wreck—women isolated from any meaningful participation or voice in forces that led to the disaster—are in a position to write its epitaph and their own names in new books. She describes a brave new world of women.

> The rules break like a thermometer,
> quicksilver spills across the charted systems,
> we're out in a country that has no language
> no laws, we're chasing the raven and the wren
> through gorges unexplored since dawn
> whatever we do together is pure invention

the maps they gave us were out of date
by years . . .

. . . .

the music on the radio comes clear—
neither *Rosenkavalier* nor *Götterdämmerung*
but a woman's voice singing old songs
with new words, with a quiet bass, a flute
plucked and fingered by women outside the law.
("Twenty-One Love Poems" XIII)

Rich's major transformation is in turning away from the despair engendered by an isolation of women enforced by men toward the energy and prophecy of an isolation chosen by women. Isolation is no
longer seen as marginality of self and separation from strength, but as
a fiercely willed rejection of the ruined and ruining heritage of the destructive, defrauded androcentric culture.

Could you imagine a world of women only,
the interviewer asked. *Can you imagine*

a world where women are absent. (He believed
he was joking.) Yet I have to imagine

at one and the same moment, both. Because
I live in both. *Can you imagine,*

the interviewer asked, *a world of men?*
(He thought he was joking.) *If so, then,*

a world where men are absent?
Absently, wearily, I answered: Yes.

. . . .

It was never the crude pestle, the blind
ramrod we were after:

merely a fellow-creature
with natural resources equal to our own

Meanwhile, another kind of being
was constructing itself, blindly

—a mutant, some have said:
the blood-compelled exemplar

of a "botched civilization"
as one of them called it
a child picking up guns
for that is what it means to be a man

. . . .

and that kind of being has lain in our beds
declaring itself our desire

requiring women's blood for life
a woman's breast to lay its nightmare on.
("Natural Resources")

In the poem, "Waking in the Dark," Rich writes:

The tragedy of sex
lies around us, a woodlot
the axes are sharpened for.

. . . .

A man's world. But finished.
They themselves have sold it to the machines.
I walk the unconscious forest
a woman dressed in old army fatigues
that have shrunk to fit her

. . . .

Nothing will save this. I am alone,
kicking the last rotting logs
with their strange smell of life, not death,
wondering what on earth it all might have become.

Through their ancient and unnatural existence on the boundaries of "patriarchal space" (as Mary Daly terms it), women are freer to escape the terminal fragmentation of the collapsing patriarchy. At this moment of historical transition, as Rich conceives it, the male cultural configurations are falling in upon themselves, leaving women as the legitimate creators of new forms. Through women's rediscovery of connection and solidarity, their traditional isolation emerges no longer as weakness, paralysis, or spiritual death, but as the basis of a profound power through the sharing of vision and love.

> . . . you, fellow-creature, sister,
> sitting across from me, dark with love,
> working like me to pick apart
> working with me to remake
> this trailing knitted thing, this cloth of darkness,
> this women's garment, trying to save the skein.
> ("When We Dead Awaken")

> . . . *Now we are ready*
> *and each of us knows it   I have never loved*
> *like this   I have never seen*
> *my own forces so taken up and shared*
> *and given back*
>
> . . . .
>
> *We know now we have always been in danger*
> *down in our separateness*
> *and now up here together   but till now*
> *we had not touched our strength*
> ("Phantasia for Elvira Shatayev")

Rich writes of her poetic direction: "It is not interesting to me to explore the condition of alienation as a woman as it is to explore the condition of connectedness as a woman. Which is something absolutely new, unique historically, and which is finally so much more life-enhancing—it doesn't lead to a static or doomed notion of the universe. What I finally began to give up on in the poetry of many of my male contemporaries at a certain point is this sense that we're all doomed to fail somehow."[27] As the feminist critic Erica Jong has written of Rich's recent work,

> The poems are not only about dead ends. They are about loneliness and the various forms it takes: the loneliness of being an artist, an outsider, a survivor. Human loneliness is one of the

27. Grimstad and Rennie, *Sourcebook,* 106.

great themes in all the arts, and Adrienne Rich depicts it more intensely than in any other recent book I know. But she also shows that loneliness can be the beginning of rebirth. The woman, because she stands outside the death-dealing culture and its power games, can be a visionary who points the way to redemption: about sister giving birth to sister, and woman giving birth to herself.[28]

"Life-enhancing," "visionary," "up here together . . . touch[ing] our strength," all are clear expressions of validation. Rich's theme concerns the validation of women's experiences as imperatives for the quality and continuation of life, the expression of their truths, and the discovery of their power and their connection to themselves and each other. Involved is a tremendous process of renaming, reducing language to its essentials, burning away the distortions of words rendered in what Rich calls "the oppressor's language," which has distorted the way reality is perceived.[29]

> But there come times—perhaps this is one of them—
> when we have to take ourselves more seriously or die;
> when we have to pull back from the incantations,
> rhythms we've moved to thoughtlessly
> and disenthrall ourselves, bestow
> ourselves to silence, or a deeper listening, cleansed
> of oratory, formulas, choruses, laments, static
> crowding the wires. We cut the wires,
>
> . . . .
>
> No one who survives to speak
> new language, has avoided this:
> the cutting away of an old force that held her
> rooted to an old ground
> ("Transcendental Etude")

28. Erica Jong, "Visionary Anger," in Gelpi and Gelpi (eds.), *Adrienne Rich's Poetry*, 173.

29. Rich voiced the opinion to an interviewer that "the first thing an oppressor tries to do is take away the culture from the oppressed—change their language, change their lifestyle, repress their art, denigrate it, trivialize it. This is the first political weapon after the gun." Grimstad and Rennie, *Sourcebook*, 109.

Our whole life a translation
the permissible fibs

and now a knot of lies
eating at itself to get done

Words bitten through words

meanings burnt-off like paint
under the blowtorch

All those dead letters
rendered into the oppressor's language
("Our Whole Life")

"Song," a poem of validation, refashions the meaning of loneliness, re-interprets isolation to refer to those whose position is in the forefront of a new order rather than to those left behind.

You're wondering if I'm lonely:
OK then, yes, I'm lonely
as a plane rides lonely and level
on its radio beam, aiming
across the Rockies
for the blue-strung aisles
of an airfield on the ocean

You want to ask, am I lonely?
Well, of course, lonely
as a woman driving across country
day after day, leaving behind
mile after mile
little towns she might have stopped
and lived and died in, lonely

If I'm lonely
it must be the loneliness
of waking first, of breathing
dawn's cold breath on the city
of being the one awake
in a house wrapped in sleep

> If I'm lonely
> it's with the rowboat ice-fast on the shore
> in the last red light of the year
> that knows what it is, that knows it's neither
> ice nor mud nor winter light
> but wood, with a gift for burning
> ("Song")

The rhetorical structure poses conventional, self-diminishing views of loneliness against those of power, intensity, and necessity; the speaker is isolated only as far as her passion and lucidity have propelled her. She goes farther out on the frontiers of human possibilities than those around her. The issue of language and isolation is also addressed in "The Stranger," concluding in a prophecy of new myths.

> if I come into a room out of the sharp misty light
> and hear them talking a dead language
> if they ask me my identity
> what can I say but
> I am the androgyne
> I am the living mind you fail to describe
> in your dead language
> the lost noun, the verb surviving
> only in the infinitive
> the letters of my name are written under the lids
> of the newborn child.

The creation of myths necessitates a basic shift in Rich's voice from that of her own private, local instance to the voice of all women. Part of her effort is to retrieve women from history, touch their strength, and give them back to us as our models; her poems remind us of Marie Curie, Caroline Herschel, Natalya Gorbanevskaya, Paula Becker, Elvira Shatayev, and others. It is a sign of her extraordinary power as a poet that Rich is able to speak movingly with a voice of such magnitude, empathy, and range. "From an Old House in America," is a *tour de force*, fusing the experience of American women, regardless of century, color, or locale, into a prototype of their tale.

I am an American woman:
I turn that over

like a leaf pressed in a book
I stop and look up from

into the coals of the stove
or the black square of the window

Foot-slogging through the Bering Strait
jumping from the *Arbella* to my death

chained to the corpse beside me
I feel my pains begin

I am washed up on this continent
shipped here to be fruitful

my body a hollow ship
bearing sons to the wilderness

sons who ride away
on horseback, daughters

whose juices drain like mine
into the arroyo of stillbirths, massacres

Hanged as witches, sold as breeding wenches
my sisters leave me

I am not the wheatfield
nor the virgin forest

I never chose this place
yet I am of it now

. . . .

I have lived in isolation
from other women, so much

The lyrical, beautiful "Planetarium" similarly moves from the individual life of a woman to the lives of women, as Rich assumes the identity of the mythic goddesses configuring the sky with their tales. The first few lines address the ancient distortion of women by men who named the universe, who persisted in finding something monstrous and punishable in women's power and freedom.

A woman in the shape of a monster
a monster in the shape of a woman
the skies are full of them

. . . .

Galaxies of women, there
doing penance for impetuousness
ribs chilled
in those spaces of the mind

Rich draws her inspiration from the work of a woman astronomer, Caroline Herschel, whose life was dedicated to mapping the universe. Rich feels Herschel's imperative to pioneer in a new discovery—a discovery of the patterns of women's lives. Her stance is tough, resilient, and fully committed: "I am bombarded yet   I stand." The radio signals that bombard her are the male (Taurus) languages that have previously tried to name the world.

The radio impulse
pouring in from Taurus

            I am bombarded yet   I stand

I have been standing all my life in the
direct path of a battery of signals
the most accurately transmitted most
untranslateable language in the universe
I am a galactic cloud so deep so invo-
luted that a light wave could take 15
years to travel through me   And has
taken   I am an instrument in the shape
of a woman trying to translate pulsations
into images   for the relief of the body
and the reconstruction of the mind.

As a poet committed to re-creation and the possibilities of life, she must "translate" this "most untranslateable language" into "images" for the "relief of the body / and the reconstruction of the mind." The last line echoes the conclusion of "Leaflets," in which Rich was "thinking of how we can use what we have / to invent what we need." The power and energy she feels for this task are registered by the great expanse of her image: "I am a galactic cloud so deep . . . that a light wave could take 15 years to travel through me." It is an image of women's presence and determination on an order rarely found in any poetry.

"Planetarium" is important for its implied "reconstruction" of images from earlier poems. It reinterprets the fearful female specter of "monster" and also reconciles the split-self of "Orion," which had been based on the false identification of the speaker with "cold and egotistical" masculine qualities. Numerous other poems through Rich's collections are addressed to her actual and spiritual sisters in ways that link split-selves. As she writes in "Transcendental Etude,"

> . . . I am the lover and the loved,
> home and wanderer, she who splits
> firewood and she who knocks, a stranger
> in the storm, two women, eye to eye
> measuring each other's spirit, each other's
> limitless desire,
>
> > a whole new poetry beginning here.

In his comparison of the historical perspectives of Robert Lowell and Adrienne Rich, the critic David Kalstone makes the interesting observation that Rich "refuses to be paralyzed by what she has understood," while Lowell and many contemporary male poets are paralyzed, as Rich herself points out.[30] The fragmentation and destruction of the patriarchal world around her do not turn her toward a poetry of elegy, lament, or despair.

> *This is what I am*: watching the spider
> rebuild—"patiently," they say,
>
> but I recognize in her
> impatience—my own—
>
> the passion to make and make again
> where such unmaking reigns

30. David Kalstone, *Five Temperaments* (New York, 1977), 137.

> the refusal to be a victim
> ("Natural Resources")

Her ability to grasp a fundamental historical, mythological, and psychological isolation from the patriarchal culture—an isolation that had earlier overwhelmed her—now appears as the basis of freedom energizing a poetry of new vision. If isolation from the male-dominated world has been women's curse, then Rich believes that upon the ruins of that world women can turn their integrity to the task of building a new world.

> They can rule the world while they persuade us
> our pain belongs in some order.
> .   .   .   .
> yes, that male god that acts on us and on our children,
> that male state that acts on us and our children
> till our brains are blunted by malnutrition,
> yet sharpened by the passion for survival,
> our powers expended daily on the struggle
> to hand a kind of life on to our children,
> to change reality for our lovers
> even in a single trembling drop of water.
> .   .   .   .
>   We shrink from touching
> our power, we shrink away, we starve ourselves
> and each other, we're scared shitless
> of what it could be to take and use our love,
> hose it on a city, on a world
> to wield and guide its spray . . .
> . . . like the terrible mothers we long and dread to be.
> ("Hunger")

Rich's political and sexual direction has led her increasingly toward the concept of female bonding as the truest expression of validation— the love of women for women in a final turning away from the failures of the old patterns. Again, she draws upon the refashioning and rediscovery of myth to give herself a foundation.

> The daughters never were
> true brides of the father

the daughters were to begin with
brides of the mother

then brides of each other
under a different law

Let me hold and tell you
("Sibling Mysteries")

Birth stripped our birthright from us,
tore us from a woman, from women, from ourselves
so early on
and the whole chorus throbbing at our ears
like midges, told us nothing, nothing
of origins, nothing we needed
to know, nothing that could re-member us.
("Transcendental Etude")

Her images for validation have also continued to take the form of space and height and freedom, reversing the imagery of victimization, its opposite; she uses constellations, radio beams, helicopters, and mountain peaks. Nowhere is her imagery more movingly depicted, the coming together of women in their isolation and power more beautifully drawn than in the incredible poem "Phantasia for Elvira Shatayev," from her collection *The Dream of a Common Language* (1977). Shatayev was the leader of a women's mountain climbing expedition that perished during a storm at the summit of a mountain in the Caucasus; Shatayev's husband followed to bury the bodies. Rich uses their climb as a metaphor for women's discovery of a desire and beauty they could never find in the world below.

The cold felt cold until our blood
grew colder   then the wind
died down and we slept

If in this sleep I speak
it's with a voice no longer personal
(I want to say   *with voices*)
When the wind tore   our breath from us at last
we had no need of words
For months   for years   each one of us

had felt her own *yes*   growing in her
slowly forming   as she stood at windows   waited
for trains   mended her rucksack   combed her hair
What we were to learn   was simply   what we had
up here   as out of all words   that *yes*   gathered
its forces   fused itself   and only just in time
to meet a *No* of no degrees
the black hole   sucking the world in

I feel you climbing toward me
your cleated bootsoles leaving   their geometric bite
colossally embossed   on microscopic crystals
as when I trailed you in the Caucasus
Now I am further
ahead   than either of us dreamed   anyone would be
I have become

the white snow packed like asphalt by the wind
the women I love   lightly flung   against the mountain
that blue sky
our frozen eyes unribboned   through the storm
we could have stitched that blueness   together   like
      a quilt

You come (I know this)   with our love   your loss
strapped to your body   with your tape-recorder   camera
ice-pick   against advisement
to give us burial in the snow   and in your mind
While my body lies out here
flashing like a prism into your eyes
how could you sleep   You climbed here for yourself
we climbed for ourselves

When you have buried us   told your story
ours does not end   we stream
into the unfinished   the unbegun
the possible
Every cell's core of heat   pulsed out of us
into the thin air   of the universe
the armature of rock beneath these snows

this mountain   which has taken   the imprint of our minds
through changes elemental and minute
as those we underwent
to bring each other here
choosing ourselves   each other   and this life
whose every breath   and grasp   and further foothold
is somewhere still enacted   and continuing

In the diary I wrote: *Now we are ready*
and each of us knows it   I have never loved
like this   I have never seen
my own forces so taken up and shared
and given back
After the long training   the early sieges
We are moving almost effortlessly in our love

In the diary as the wind began   to tear
at the tents over us   I wrote
We know we have always been in danger
down in our separateness
and now up here together   but till now
we had not touched our strength

In the diary torn from my fingers I had written
what does love mean
what does it mean   "to survive"
A cable of blue fire ropes our bodies
burning together in the snow   We will not live
to settle for less. We have dreamed of this
all of our lives

Adrienne Rich wrote recently,

If someone were to ask me, "What do you hope for in a feminist book?" I would say: "A book which demands of us activity,
not passivity; which enlarged our sense of the female presence
in the world; a book which uses language and sensual imagery
to impart a new vision of reality, from a woman-centered loca-
tion; a book which expands our sense of the connections among
us in the bonds of history; a book which drives us wild, that is,

helps us break out from tameness and repetition into new tra-
jectories of our own."[31]

She has charted her own genius in poetry. Her work has traveled from
successive collections through each stage of women's isolation—victimization, personalization, split-self, and validation. Rich's poetry has
developed from a derivative morbidity and *huis clos* expressing an incipient, encoded sense of women's entrapment and limitation by gender (*A Change of World, The Diamond Cutters*). Her work has moved
through an emerging recognition of the personal, social, and political
forces acting upon her feminine experience (*Snapshots of a Daughter-in-
Law, Necessities of Life, Leaflets*) into the activity and creation of a female
presence in the world that has only begun to be explored and released
of its power and vision (*The Will to Change, Diving into the Wreck, The
Dream of a Common Language*).

> Who is here. The Erinyes.
> One to sit in judgment.
>
> One to speak tenderness.
> One to inscribe the verdict on the canyon wall.
>
> If you have not confessed
> the damage
>
> if you have not recognized
> the Mother of reparations
>
> if you have not come to terms
> with the inscription
>
> the terms of the ordeal
> the discipline   the verdict
>
> if still you are on your way
> still She awaits your coming.
> ("From an Old House in America")

31. Adrienne Rich, Review of *Woman and Nature* by Susan Griffin, in *New Women's Feminist Review* (November, 1978), 5.

CONCLUSION

**We are in the middle of an immense metamorphosis here, a metamor-
phosis which will, it is devoutly to be hoped, rob us of our myths and give
us back our history, which will destroy our attitudes and give us back our
personalities.**
JAMES BALDWIN, quoted by Roy Harvey Pearce
The Continuity of American Poetry

Isolation must be regarded as a major force acting on women. It embraces the private and the public, the psychic and the physical, the
given and the chosen conditions of their existence. Women's lives cannot be fully understood without our awareness of the degree and nature of the isolation they experience, nor can the poetry written by
women be viewed comprehensively without taking into account the insistence and manifestation of this theme. At the least, isolation provides a key to a fundamental reinterpretation of four poets' work.

The tension and confessionalism in Louise Bogan's poetry cannot
be viewed apart from her obsession with isolation from time, nature,
gender, and self. Her concern with uniquely feminine marginality only
begins to come clear with this additional perspective. New subtleties in
the privateness of Maxine Kumin's poetry emerge, as a sense of physical and spiritual isolation extends the complexity and meaning of her
poems on the nature of family bonds and women's experience. When
the theme of isolation is explored in Denise Levertov's work, the depth
of grief and pain takes on unprecedented power, and counterbalances
the prevailing view of her as a joyous, celebratory poet of sensual, sexual themes instead of a poet with interest in exploring the nature of
gender. Adrienne Rich's poetry similarly cannot be encompassed without understanding the radicalism of her position on women's isolation.

At best, a study of isolation among women poets provides ground
for analysis and synthesis across a diversity of styles and themes. The
imagery of enclosure, for instance, as a consistent indicator of isolation, recurs so frequently throughout women's writing that it can be
considered nearly archetypal. Similarly, the split-self emerges as a
uniquely feminine expression of inner gender division. The effort to
controvert myth and redefine experience is also intimately connected
to a woman poet's sense of isolation from the past, from culture, and
even from language.

From the prisoned cricket in a granite hill to the self-transforming freedom of women climbers on a mountain peak, the nature of isolation develops through the four visions—victimization, personalization, split-self, and validation—from a symptom and condition of weakness to a strategy of identification and strength of self. The isolation these women feel in their knowledge and experience becomes redefined and redirected in a continual movement toward greater freedom and a sense of identification through the distinction and positive significance of their separateness.

Thus, the personae of victimization poems tend to be women who took on most completely and passively the role society gave them—selfless mothers, submissive wives and lovers, dutiful dependents—but for whom the role has broken down, leaving them resigned and embittered. Because their inner selves often appear too attenuated and weak to change course with any confidence or purpose, they express the most negative isolation and sense of self. The poetic manifestation of this state is captured by Bogan's landscapes of late fall and winter, rocky terrain, barren fields and distraught humanity. Reflecting the feeling of isolation from time and possibility, hers is a poetry of effects, aftermaths, and doomed situations. In her reduced vision, the embattled inner female self constantly struggles against betrayal and death at the hands of nature, love, and the capricious physical self. These, by their unruliness and ultimate sterility, assault the rigor and sanctity of the spirit. Unable to alter the damning fact of feminine gender, the women of Bogan's poems seem unable to alter the world which is determined for them by that fact. Thematically, poems of victimization are concerned with the powerless, disillusioned self who exists in a dark, inscrutable order she finds too bleak or threatening to explore. Emotionally and physically she retreats. Consistently, Bogan's stylistic and imagistic techniques produce a single-mood poetry of despair that obstructs any dialectic of counterpointing emotions or themes, such as those achieved by poets in other stances. In the work of other poets, such a structural movement presupposes a potential for alternative outcomes that would be inconsistent with Bogan's fatalism and isolation.

If and when this negative voice is able to change, it moves in the direction of personalization, usually turning to the shaping, individual past of family and heritage in order to understand the contextual and personal aspects of gender. The bitterness in the earlier voice tends to lessen as a greater flexibility and sense of transition enter in, along with the possibility of choice and logic in one's fate. In many ways, Kumin's poems of personalization continue the themes and formal concerns of Bogan's—the threatening forces of disintegration, the tenuousness of happiness and certainty of loss, the omnipresence of death—but the isolation is not as extensive as it is in Bogan's poetry. The understanding of heritage and feminine context gives Kumin's poems more feeling of connection with other women than is ever found in Bogan's victimization poems. Also, the primarily human and interpersonal basis for isolation allows Kumin to avoid the isolation from nature that Bogan tends to feel. Kumin is able to find in a rural, natural existence a foundation for the literal and psychic movement toward self-sufficiency that lies at the heart of her poetry. The importance of nature for Kumin is seen in the extent to which she makes it vivid and tangible; indeed, her poetic signature is the immediately apt, perceptive phrase that captures this nonhuman world she turns to for solace and meaning. Kumin finds in a vigorously physical life her antidotes to the continually threatening human disintegration and loss. Like Bogan, she constantly battles the specter of death in its literal form and in its symbolic form of an emotional estrangement that seems to work its way into the closest of human bonds—mother and daughter, wife and husband, woman and woman. She cannot escape these apprehensions, but at least she is able to find a day-to-day quittance in the cyclic rhythms of the seasons and in the dignity of independent work. Kumin does not seek to control nature as Bogan does, nor to make it an emotional colony of the mind. The marshaling of things and details simply acts as a barrier against darker musings, and staves off what she calls the "history of loss." Nature presents to her an immediate order and reliability that stand in contrast to the disorder and pain of human existence. Therefore, she most often pictures a live, vital earth whose landscapes span all season, and her themes stress the importance of place, particularly the New England farm that embodies the values of earned survival, self-reliance, and renewal. Nature presents a realm that can be appealed to and explored for an alternative to the human realm, allowing for possibilities absent from Bogan's perspective.

Particularly in her recent poetry Kumin has moved beyond a poetry

of statements and didacticism into forms that operate more as exploratory vehicles. There is flexibility in the speaker's direction or action. In
contrast, Bogan wrote poems of foregone conclusions in which action,
or even the basis for action, was irrelevant. There could be little point
to personal or social action in a world of such fixed coordinates.
Kumin, however, writes poems that are open enough to incorporate a
process of definition and decision, but that do not necessarily lead to a
sense of meaningful impact on one's world. In the long run, she shares
with Bogan too great a consciousness of human helplessness and
pessimism.

   Nevertheless, in Kumin's poems, isolation begins to take on associa-
tions of resource and choice that intensify with the split, so evident in
Levertov's poems, between the acceptably integrated woman and the
marginal artist self. Increasingly, a direction emerges in which isolation is a symptom of, and means to, a mystery and power identified as
the artist's natural realm. Levertov's ambivalence toward this realm is
revealed in repeated imagery of coldness, darkness, and exotic trappings, signifying her fear and reluctance to accept in her own self the
artist as woman and the environment this demands. Yet she also reveals her need to move in this direction. Her victory is to heal the divergent selves into a concept of wholeness that accepts the woman as
woman and the woman as artist with no unnatural polarization between them, and to exist in a willed and fruitful isolation. The split in
the self stems from limiting and falsifying definitions in the society
around her, which will not allow full self-determination to women.

   The political implications of the split-self are explored with the
most power and urgency by the validation poems of Adrienne Rich,
who gives women's traditional isolation its most positive, liberating potential. In her last collections, Rich moves beyond victimization, personalization, and the split-self, into a view of women's isolation that
builds on her political and sexual synthesis to affirm a vision of validation. Her earlier poetry explored the private experience of an individual American woman; now she is moving into the mythic dimension of
women's experience as a comprehensive pattern of existing in and relating to the world. She is now many women and speaks with a voice
approaching prophecy. Her central thesis is that women can turn the
isolation and marginality they have known into the basis for a new

world. Through their powers which have yet to be tapped, their stories which are all to be told, women are at the brink of a new world. Their isolation from a male-centered culture has been a curious means of freedom. Existing on the boundaries of the patriarchy, women must preserve that isolation from dehumanization and desensitization.

Behind many of the distinctions we can draw between the poets is the sense each has of the power of the poet and of poetry itself. This view of the self as poet is connected to the degree to which that self is involved—in regard to body, space, and time—in the world. In other words, the degree of isolation a poet feels is parallel to her sense of the power of poetry. Thus Bogan, as the most isolated, has the least belief in the power of poetry or of herself as poet. Kumin's own high degree of physical and social retreat corresponds to a view of poetry that does not carve out much power for itself. However, Levertov and Rich ascribe maximum importance to poetry and to their own roles as priest or shaman.

In Bogan's essay, "The Springs of Poetry," the occasion for poetry is described as a moment of weakness and torment when all else has failed to divert the emotion. The poet is victimized by the poem, reluctant to go through the anguish and pain of revelation. For Kumin, poetry is "the little tale that's left" ("Life's Work"). "We are, each of us, our own / prisoner. We are / locked up in our own story" ("Address to the Angels"). For her, poetry bestows a personal benefit of release and recognition, but cannot summon a more powerful impact on others. Much more dramatic is the role Levertov claims for art and the artist. "We should remember the ritual, sacramental roots of art and realize that the act of creating a work of art is in its nature a celebration of life . . . and that the artist himself has a function not very different from that of priest or shaman."[1] For Rich, less mystical than Levertov but just as extensive in her conviction of the poet's scope, the poet is the ultimate revolutionary. In a world where naming is power, the poet's imperative to describe and name is the most potentially dangerous and liberating of all acts. In the ghazal "8/8/68" she wrote, "From here on, all of us will be living / like Galileo turning his first tube at the stars." In a poem written just weeks earlier, Rich concluded:

1. Denise Levertov, "Asking the Fact for the Form," cited in Linda Wagner, *Denise Levertov* (New York, 1967), 52.

Last night you wrote on the wall: Revolution is poetry.
Today you needn't write; the wall has tumbled down.

We were taught to respect the appearance behind the reality.
Our senses were out on parole, under surveillance.

A pair of eyes imprisoned for years inside my skull
is burning its way outward, the headaches are terrible.
("7/26/68: i")

A critic adds, "Many poets, probably most poets, in America today are
writing *about* revolution. The poetry of Adrienne Rich *is* revolution.
In its actual methodological progress it denies the older humanist concept of the world of imagination as separate from or contrary to ordinary reality; it shows the poem at work not only as part of reality but as
a creating and transforming part."[2]

By examining women's poetry in light of the theme of isolation, we
see a tremendously important unity existing among different styles,
periods, and concerns: the unifying belief that women's lives have
been distinct, separate and divided, and that much of women's potential has never come to its destined and necessary fulfillment. Ironically
it is the inherent potential suggested by this belief that most clearly dis-
tinguishes much male and female poetry at this time. In many cases
women poets possess a far greater conviction of optimism, a feeling of
new and necessary directions, than do many male poets, who seem
mired in rehearsals of disintegration. The frustration evident in
poetry by men seemingly signals the exhaustion of possibilities, while
the alternate excitement and frustration in women's poetry suggests
the energy for things yet untried. As Patricia Meyer Spacks asserts,
"Women dominate their own experience by imagining it, giving it
form, writing about it. Their imaginative visions of themselves as . . .
guardians of the species, possessors of wisdom unavailable to men—
visions derived partly from the arrogance of anger—in effect recreate
the 'mighty female deity.' In their exact recording of inner and outer
experience they establish women's claim for attention as individuals.

2. Hayden Carruth, "Adrienne Rich," in James Vinson and D. L. Kirkpatrick (eds.),
Contemporary Poets (2nd ed.; New York, 1975), 1271.

They define, for themselves, and for their readers, woman as she is and as she dreams."[3]

At the end of his major study, *The Continuity of American Poetry*, Roy Harvey Pearce expressed his belief that the central traditions of our (male) poetry—the Adamic and mythic modes—taken to their furthest expression in the poetry of Wallace Stevens and T.S. Eliot, had reached a dead end. Pearce stated that the task for poets in our time is to find new modes of reconciliation through new forms. That was in 1961, on the verge of a tremendous explosion in women's poetry: Anne Sexton's *To Bedlam and Part Way Back*, in 1960; Sylvia Plath's *Ariel*, in 1961; Maxine Kumin's first book, in 1961; Denise Levertov's *O Taste and See*, in 1962; Rich's *Snapshots of a Daughter-in-Law*, in 1963; and the revival of the poets whose work broke important ground earlier. At present, women poets would seem to have the best chance of escaping the exhaustion and collapse of the Adamic and mythic modes, never having truly felt at the center of that world nor having had the truths of their experience described and encompassed by the tales of the tribe. Rich feels this strongly in her own and other women's work, the sense that women's poetry essentially confronts the despairing wasteland tradition of male poetry because of a distance from the civilization it depicts in collapse. She writes in regard to H.D.'s *Trilogy* that the poet is "not mourning the collapse of Western civilization but turning back for inspiration to prehistory, to a gynocentric tradition. H.D. insisted that the poet-as-woman should stop pouring her energies into a ground left sterile. . . . 'Let us leave / the place-of-skull / to them that have made it.'"[4] Elsewhere, Rich writes further on this redirection in women's poetry. "I have thought that the sense of doom and resignation to loneliness endemic in much masculine poetry has to do with a sense of *huis clos*, of having come to the end of a certain kind of perception. What I would like to offer here is a clue to a way onward, a way that will of necessity dredge up much wretchedness, but that will, I believe, be finally transfiguring."[5]

3. Patricia Meyer Spacks, *The Female Imagination* (New York, 1972), 413–14.
4. Adrienne Rich, "Power and Danger: Words of a Common Woman," in Rich, *On Lies, Secrets and Silence: Selected Prose 1966–1978* (New York, 1979), 238.
5. Adrienne Rich, "Poetry, Personality, and Wholeness: A Response to Galway Kinnell," *Field*, VII (1972), 18.

An enormous amount of energy and experimentation is coming out of women's poetry in our time, including a fierce optimism for the potential of human life on earth and the fulfillment of human dignity for the first time for women and men. Pearce writes: "I assume that our characteristically American commitments, aspirations and theories are by definition also those of our poets, who stand for ourselves working at full creative pitch. . . . A poet is ours to the degree that he is gifted with that kind of sensibility which will let him push to their farthest implications such possibilities (and impossibilities) for the life of the spirit as are latent in the culture of his—and our—community, past and present."[6] It is women who are everywhere emerging as "our poets"; in their vigorous new visions of our patterns of human experience and the meaning of humanity, they exemplify a commitment to the ideal Pearce articulates. I believe women's poetry today is very much in the tradition of American poetry and that it is moving in the direction of the new sense of *communitas* Pearce predicted would need to come, moving toward new ways of understanding and realizing human dignity, which he identifies as the American poet's continuous theme.

6. Roy Harvey Pearce, *The Continuity of American Poetry*, (Princeton, N.J., 1961), 10.

INDEX

Abishag, 8. *See also* Myths
Adamic mode, 9, 169
Advantage of Lyric, The, 48
Alexander, Curt, 24–28 *passim*
Alexander, Mathilde (Maidie), 28, 43
Altérité, 8
Anderson, Maxwell, 28*n*9
Arachne, 61. *See also* Myth
Ariel. See Plath, Sylvia
Auden, Wystan Hugh, 49, 117, 121–23

Beach, Joseph, 12
Beauvoir, Simone de, 8, 56
Bernikow, Louise, 3
Berryman, John, 7
Becker, Paula Modersohn, 154
Bildungsroman, 6
Bogan, Daniel, 24–28
Bogan, Louise: 8, 9, 10, 15–53, 66, 81, 141, 163–67
—life of: childhood of, 24–28; parents of, 24–28 *passim*; marriage of, to Curt Alexander, 24–28 *passim*; marriage of, to Raymond Holden, 42, 43; daughter (Mathilde) of, 28, 43; on her Irishness, 26; drinking problems of, 42, 52; financial struggles of, 28, 43; honors won by, 43, 52; mental illness of, 42–48 *passim*, 52–53; and Theodore Roethke, 28, 43; last years of, 52–53
—views and devices of: view of nature, 16, 17, 18–23 *passim*, 25, 40, 51, 164–65; use of female myth figures, 21, 29–31, 36, 41–42, 44–47 *passim*, 50–51; view of poetry, 27–28, 44–45; victimization, 10, 15–24 *passim*, 29–34 *passim*, 40, 44, 47–48, 52; split-self, 16, 50; personalization, 48–50; validation, 50
—books of: *Body of This Death*, 15, 17, 18–24 *passim*, 28, 38, 40, 41, 52, 59; *Dark Summer*, 17, 40, 42; *The Sleeping Fury*, 17, 43, 52; *Poems and New Poems*, 17, 43; *Collected Poems*, 43, 52; *The Blue Estuaries*, 17, 43; *What the Woman Lived: Selected Letters*, 24*n*7; *Journey Around My Room, A Mosaic*, 25*n*8

—poems of: "Ad Castitatem," 24, 29–31, 36; "After the Persian," 17, 50–51; "At a Party," 44; "Baroque Comment," 43*n*11; "Beginning and End," 24*n*6, 41; "Betrothed," 19, 21–24, 28; "Cassandra," 41–42; "The Changed Woman," 36–37; "Chanson un peu naive," 37; "The Crossed Apple," 50; "The Crows," 32, 36, 50; "The Cupola," 41; "The Daemon," 47; "Dark Summer," 41, 49; "Decoration," 18; "Didactic Piece," 41; "The Dream," 29, 46–47; "The Drum," 41; "Elders," 24*n*6; "Evening in the Sanitarium," 49–50; "Feuernacht," 41; "Fiend's Weather," 41; "Fifteenth Farewell," 38–39; "The Frightened Man," 18, 19, 35–36; "Heard by a Girl," 49; "Henceforth from the Mind," 44; "Homunculus," 44; Hypocrite Swift," 42; "If We Take All Gold," 41; "I Saw Eternity," 41; "Italian Morning," 44; "Kept," 48; "Knowledge," 18, 24, 30, 37; "Last Hill in a Vista," 34–36, 38; "Late," 41; "A Letter," 18, 35, 41; "Little Lobelia's Song," 49; "Man Alone," 44; "Medusa," 18, 20–21, 35; "Men Loved Wholly Beyond Wisdom," 19, 24, 32, 37; "My Voice Not Being Proud," 18; "Packet of Letters," 44; "Poem in Prose," 44; "Portrait," 18, 24, 30–31; "Resolve," 24*n*6; "Roman Fountain," 44; "Second Song," 41; "Short Summary," 44; "Single Sonnet," 4; "Simple Autumnal," 41; "The Sleeping Fury," 44, 45–47, 49, 50; "Song for a Lyre," 44; "Song for the Last Act," 17; "Sonnet," 39–40; "Stanza," 36; "Statue and Birds," 18, 31–32, 33, 50; "The Stones," 24*n*6; "Survival," 24*n*6, 41; "A Tale," 18–20, 35; "To a Dead Lover," 24*n*6; "To Wine," 44; "Winter Swan," 40–41, 50; "Women," 10, 19, 33–34, 36; "Words for Departure," 19, 24, 36, 41; "The Young Wife," 24*n*6, 28, 41
—essays of: "July Dawn" (folio), 48*n*14; "The Springs of Poetry," 44, 47, 167